AROUND THE WORLD IN
SALADS

AROUND THE WORLD IN
SALADS

120 ways to love your leaves

Katie & Giancarlo Caldesi

Photography by Helen Cathcart

Kyle Books

To Manjula, thank you for four wonderful years,
we wish you every success for the future.

First published in Great Britain in 2016 by
Kyle Books
an imprint of Kyle Cathie Limited
192–198 Vauxhall Bridge Road
London SW1V 1DX
general.enquiries@kylebooks.co.uk
www.kylebooks.co.uk

10 9 8 7 6 5 4 3 2 1

ISBN: 978 0 85783 302 0

A CIP catalogue record for this title is available from the British
Library

Jicama Salad by Jane Milton on page 184 from *The Practical
Encyclopedia of Mexican Cooking* © Anness Publishing Ltd

Editor: Vicky Orchard
Design: Louise Leffler
Photography: Helen Cathcart
Food styling: Susie Theodorou
Props styling: Linda Berlin
Production: Gemma John and Nic Jones

Colour reproduction by ALTA London
Printed and bound in China by 1010 International Printing Ltd.

Nutritional information key:

 – dairy free

 – gluten-free

 – vegetarian

 – vegan

contents

introduction

I have always been drawn to salads; I like the crunch of fresh vegetables, lively colourful leaves and punchy dressings. They sharpen my mind and give me energy yet still fill me up without leaving me sluggish and tired. I can't say the same for how my husband, Giancarlo, feels; he was pasta man and I was salad girl. Then within one month our world turned upside down. Giancarlo was told he was diabetic; he had to lose weight, give up sugar and eat less carbohydrates. This meant less pasta, no more cappuccino with sugar or cakes and biscuits. Then just weeks later he was told he was intolerant to gluten, badly so. Poor Giancarlo! He had to give up pasta, bread and pizza, all the things a traditional Italian man loves. On the bright side, he could eat salad and no one told him he shouldn't eat vegetables!

Months after this we found out that our son Giorgio is also gluten intolerant; he had been experiencing headaches, migraines and moments when he was so tired and weak he couldn't get up. So now we are pretty much gluten-free as a family and vegetables take centre stage. We grow plenty of our own and try to buy local and organic when they are available.

Salad is fresh, it is rich in nutrients and usually, though not exclusively, low in sugar and often gluten-free. This book, inspired by our new way of eating at home, follows the 90/10 rule in that we eat healthy food made from scratch 90 per cent of the time, treating ourselves to indulgences for the other 10 per cent. We like to eat loads of fresh vegetables, good meat and fish, wholegrains and as little sugar as possible. When we eat carbohydrates, such as pasta, potatoes, grains or sugary foods such as fresh or dried fruit, natural and processed forms of sugar, we eat them with protein and fat so as not to raise blood sugar levels. Looking back this is the way that Giancarlo's family ate in Tuscany when he was growing up. Small portions of pasta were eaten with ragù, meat went further with plenty of vegetables, and salad from the garden accompanied bread and cheese. His family were all lean and healthy. It was in the UK Giancarlo started to have huge portions of pasta, milky coffee all day, cravings for sweet fruits and sugary biscuits. To stop this I needed him and our children to cross over to the greener side of life.

Together we set out to discover new ways of eating vegetables and focused on salads from all corners of the world. We travelled to South East Asia, Morocco, Italy and the US to discover a new way of eating. We worked with family cooks and chefs from countries such as India, Nepal, Sri Lanka, Cambodia, North and South America, China, Japan, France, Kuwait, Greece, Peru, Korea and more. We wanted to understand and be confident in using unfamiliar ingredients to prepare dressings, marinades and spice rubs. We also learnt to cut vegetables differently, how presentation makes a huge difference, how to play with textures and balance sweet and sour.

From our travels we have broadened our culinary horizons. We have been inspired by other cultures and have been enthused by the people we have met, all those cooks who have generously brought their salads to life for us. We have hugely increased our repertoire of family meals and found a healthier way to eat.

Giancarlo and I are both enthusiastic teachers (in our cookery school) as well as restaurateurs. In writing this book we want to say 'look how easy this is to prepare', 'try this, it's really good for you and tastes amazing' and above all 'look how you can make everyday vegetables into a magnificent and moreish salad'.

what is a salad?

The word 'salad' comes from *herbe salato*, meaning 'salted leaves', referring to a bowl of dressed leaves, and dates back to ancient Rome and possibly before. Pliny, the ancient Roman writer, wrote to his friend about a salad kept cool with snow and reprimanded him for being too busy with dancing girls to notice this amazing phenomena.

The Italian gardener and writer Castelvetro was horrified by the eating habits of the English in the 1600s and wrote a whole book about how we should eat more salad. He didn't want us to waste the herbs and leaves around us and wanted us to use a greater variety of them. As history repeats itself, I learned of the current trend of using the whole vegetable in a recent trip to New York. Leftover parts of vegetables, such as carrot tops, beetroot leaves and broccoli stalks can be used to provide further nutrients and varying textures to make a salad far more interesting, see the carrot top crunch on page 181 and the beet leaf salad on page 130.

Salad means different things to different people. For some it means cold but then salad can be warm, it is often chopped but then a whole lettuce or whole dressed beans are still salad. Does it have to contain leaves or something raw? No, sometimes it is entirely made with cooked, dressed vegetables. We have also included a variety of dips which are not strictly salads on their own but play a big part in the whole salad picture. And there is meat, chicken and fish as well as tofu and bean salads for additional protein. To us, salads are plant-based meals and have some sort of dressing.

what makes a good salad?

Start with the ingredients. What is in the fridge and needs using? What is in season and at its prime in the shops? Perky carrots and crisp lettuce need no more than a good dressing or dip, but don't discard limp coriander, make it into Coriander Chutney (page 40) or use past-its-best parsley for Salsa Verde (page 91). Pick your ingredients from a tree or a shelf and assemble. That is salad.

textures

This is probably the most important lesson I have learned writing this book. Using a variety of textures can make a salad exciting, different and generally more loved. It is essential to find a balance between wet and dry as well as soft and crunchy. Salad appears at almost every meal now in our house, sometimes as the main event and sometimes as the supporting cast. We pull out ingredients from the fridge such as a couple of carrots, coarsely grate them into a pile, season them and squeeze a lemon over the top. I take a piece of cheese and use a peeler to make transparent shavings of it next to the carrot. We tear a little cooked chicken into shreds, pour over

the best olive oil and add sea salt flakes and freshly ground black pepper. A handful of soft leaves, slices of pepper, chewy grains or cooked beans is mixed with a few crunchy toasted seeds or nuts and a little homemade dressing. It is vibrant, fresh and balanced with plenty of varying textures. The ingredients are not necessarily tossed together, they are in piles so fussy diners can avoid peppers or coriander (you know who you are!). Supper in less than 20 minutes.

balance and sweetness – salt, spice and sugar

Salads and dressings need balance in flavour between sweet and sour. As acids such as vinegar or citrus fruits are usually involved, they are balanced with something sweet. This might be apple, dried fruit or processed sweetener. In Vietnam sugar is used to balance a sharp green lemon juice dressing. Red wine vinegar is mellowed by a teaspoon of sugar in French vinaigrette and sweet mirin balances Japanese sour flavours. We have tried to minimise these sweeteners without destroying the balance.

Where possible we have used natural sugars (as we don't like to eat processed foods) such as raw honey, maple syrup or soft dried dates – but they are still fructose- (fruit sugar) based, the same as caster or brown sugars, and will raise your blood sugar level, so should be kept to a minimum. There is no point feeling self-righteous about eliminating packet sugar from your diet and replacing it with handfuls of raisins or low-fat dressings filled with sugar. If we have used a sweetener we have used the minimum we feel the recipe needs and balanced it with protein or fat to reduce sugar spikes. Rice malt syrup is not fructose-based so do substitute this; it has a malty flavour which can be delicious but might overwhelm some dressings. Agave syrup is a good substitute for honey in a recipe if you are vegan but since it is made from the cactus plant, it is also fructose and will raise your blood sugar level if not eaten with protein or fat. Slices of peach, apple, oranges, clementines, blueberries or strawberries will add natural sweetness to a salad if needed and sharp citrus fruits such as yuzu, lemons, lime or Seville oranges offer natural acidity. Indulgent recipes such as the Pineapple & Cashew Rice Salad with Hula Pork & Roast Peppers (page 74) and the sweet salads at the end of the book are meant to be treats and not the norm.

A few textures to inspire:

Crushed peppercorns – pink, green and black

Fried capers

Bombay mix

Breadcrumbs from stale sourdough make excellent croutons
and can be flavoured with herbs, citrus or garlic

Crispy fried onions

Crunchy onions soaked in cold water to reduce strength

Little morsels of fried meats, such as bacon, chorizo or crumbled
cooked sausage

Nuts, soaked, toasted, ground, caramelised savoury and sweet,
smoky almonds

Seeds, such as pumpkin, sunflower or sesame seeds should
be toasted first to add crunch as well as flavour

Chopped pickles, such as walnuts, onions, chillies, capers and
olives to add bite

Edible flowers give colour and soft texture, if herbs have flowers
use them as well as the herb

Cheese shavings

ingredients

leaves and how to treat them nicely

There is a huge variety of leaves available, yet how many times do we see a green salad made from tasteless leaves with horrid textures? Frisse and iceberg do not make an appearance in this book. Mache or lamb's lettuce are pretty to look at but have no real flavour. I love mustard leaves, watercress and rocket, but Giancarlo finds them too peppery so I slip in a few leaves without overwhelming the other flavours in a salad and he is none the wiser. Find a variety of leaves you like and if possible grow them yourself from a salad mix of seeds. And don't forget sprouted seeds, microgreens or common or garden cress. Cress and other seedlings will reward you with a differing texture and scale to other leaves.

If you can grow your own, our friend Paolo Arrigo, who sells seeds, told me to look out for those that are bred in a similar climate to your own. He is passionate (he is Italian) about people using seeds that are developed in the same conditions they will be growing in. With cloches and seeds from colder climates we can get lettuces to last through winter. Mixed salad leaves grow so quickly, it is incredible the joy I get from wandering outside to see the day's progress; the new gardener in me is smugly content and our family eats organic green vegetables cheaply. When we lived in a flat in London an old desk became my growing table by a sunny window, so there is really no excuse for not growing just a few leaves.

It's so wasteful to throw away bags of herbs that you didn't use before they became a soggy mush, but it happens to us all. With a little thought this can be prevented. Treat them like flowers by following the tips below and they will reward you with a longer life.

Don't wash the herbs if you grew them and you know they are clean from pesticides and animal visits. For everything else you buy, wash them straight after purchasing by plunging them into a bowl or sink full of cold or ice-cold water. It will revive them and give them a much-needed drink.

Leaves should be dry for storage or use. Our salad spinner is in use most days, particularly throughout the growing season, flinging the water away from leaves via centrifugal force. It's a gadget so our kids love it and it gives them a job to do. If you don't have one, or the space to store one, loosely wrap leaves in a tea towel, clutching the ends at arm's distance. Spin it round and round outdoors and watch the drips fall on unsuspecting passers-by. Great fun and effective.

For herbs, trim the stems (and repeated every two days) and put the leaves in a container of fresh, cold water that won't fall over easily in the fridge; it could be a vase or cut plastic bottle of water. Cover loosely with a plastic or paper bag as this will give a little insulation against the cooler fridge temperature. Parsley can be either in or out of the fridge, basil is the most delicate so keeping the leaves still on the plant and out of the fridge is best. Mint is happy on a sunny windowsill. Coriander lasts better in the cooler temperature of the fridge. Hardy rosemary and thyme don't need covering but fare better in the fridge (or a cool place in the house) in water and uncovered. You can stand the container where bottles are held upright in the door of the fridge, which is usually the warmest part, too, so your herbs won't freeze.

Massage tough leaves such as kale and other obstinate cabbages with your hands for 5 minutes. They will visibly soften and brighten in colour. This will happen as the cellulose structure breaks down, a little salt, oil or lemon (or a little of each) helps the massage but it also works without.

grains

Grains are a good source of vitamins and minerals, they fill you up and give you energy as they are a blend of protein and carbohydrate. We love grains and use them often in small quantities to fill up our hungry teenage boys.

Wholegrains are best – brown rice, farro, spelt, barley, amaranth, freekeh, wheatberries, buckwheat, teff and hemp have more fibre and nutrients as none of the grain is stripped away. This means they are a slow-releasing carbohydrate and cause less of a spike in blood sugar levels. It is said the Romans won their empire on feeding their soldiers farro as it kept them fighting longer.

soaking grains, seeds and nuts

If your diet contains a significant amount of raw nuts, nut butters, unsprouted grains and seeds (which is a good way to eat, in my opinion) you should consider soaking and drying them first. This trend was started by Sally Fallon in her brilliant book *Nourishing Traditions*. In their natural state grains, seeds and nuts contain enzyme inhibitors which prevent them from sprouting when there may not be enough moisture to allow them germinate properly. Enzyme inhibitors can clog our digestive systems, giving us stomach aches. Grains particularly and nuts, to a lesser extent, contain phytic acid, goitrogens and tannins which are anti-nutrients and inhibit the absorption of minerals. Soaked and dried nuts, grains and seeds taste better, too.

By soaking nuts, grains and seeds in salted or plain water the enzyme inhibitors are neutralised, the production of beneficial enzymes and nutrients, such as vitamin B, is encouraged and proteins become broken down more easily, rendering them all the more nutritious. If you are using nuts straight after soaking there is no need to dry them but if you want to store them they must be completely dry or they will become mouldy. If they are then dried at a low temperature the nutrients are preserved. Salt helps the process along. Grains containing more phytic acid should be soaked in an acidic solution. Buckwheat contains phytase, which means it can help break down the phytic acid itself.

To do this, soak the nuts in filtered water (you can add 1 tablespoon sea salt per 4 cups nuts) in a covered container at room temperature for 12 hours. Remove and rinse the nuts thoroughly then drain them well. Spread the nuts out onto a dehydrator or oven tray. Put them into the dehydrator or oven at 45°C for 12–24 hours or until completely dry. Turn them occasionally during this time to ensure even drying. Store in an airtight container at room temperature or in the freezer to maintain their flavour better.

soaking times

Pumpkin seeds, chickpeas, black beans, mung beans, sesame seeds, sunflower seeds, almonds, aduki, amaranth, wild rice, pistachios and hazelnuts – 8–12 hours
Quinoa, walnuts, millet – 4 hours
Barley, kamut, lentils, wheatberries, buckwheat, oat groats, pecans – 6–7 hours
Cashews, Brazil nuts, pine nuts and macadamias – 2–6 hours
Flaxseed – 30 minutes

If you are in a hurry, pour boiling water over the nuts, grains or seeds and wait 10 minutes. However, you will destroy some of the beneficial nutrients as well as the enzyme inhibitors.

gluts and leftovers

Salads are a good way to use up leftovers and vegetable gluts; we love the idea of getting two or three meals from one roast. Leftover beef can be turned into Mexican beef salad (page 88), torn chicken used in an Old English Sallet (page 67) and cooked ham can become Warm Smoked Ham & Celery Salad (page 73). We make stock from the bones and have learned from our Kuwaiti friend Amal to cook grains in stock to give them more flavour. As new gardeners we still haven't managed to control gluts of produce so salads have become good ways of using up the never-ending supply of courgettes – see the Quinoa, Courgette & Corn Salad (page 185).

oil and vinegar

There is a world of various oils and vinegars on the market. Do experiment. I have to admit to being attached to extra virgin olive oil. Like a good champagne, it just makes everything a little bit better. We use an everyday extra virgin olive oil for cooking and making dressings and a more expensive single-estate oil for dressing salads and cooked foods, adding it at the last minute so that the flavour can be appreciated. Olive oil varies greatly from robust and peppery, such as a Tuscan oil, to subtle and grassy, such as a Ligurian oil. It is the same for areas of Spain and Greece, so do experiment. Rapeseed is preferred by many and it is local to us but is not our favourite flavour, however do replace olive oil with rapeseed if you prefer. Less versatile oils but just as good are walnut, hazelnut, avocado and argan; they make wonderful dressings and offer a good nutty flavour.

We don't buy flavoured oils such as orange, basil or lemon, instead we prefer to put basil leaves or grated zest in olive oil and leave it to infuse overnight. It is just as good and less costly.

We use sesame (not toasted), groundnut and grapeseed oils for Asian cooking. They have little or no flavour but are used for cooking or to help to coat leaves and other ingredients in their companion flavours in a dressing.

A refillable spray bottle of oil is especially useful if baking food. A quick spray is all you need.

Vinegars vary greatly in percentage acidity, our best tip is to take a sip of a vinegar before using it. If it chokes you with strength you will know to be cautious! If it has balance and sweetness, such as a Japanese vinegar, you know you can be liberal with it. Wine vinegars vary greatly and generally you get what you pay for. Those with named grapes, such as Sauvignon or Champagne, can be interesting and even better, homemade vinegar is lovely. Sherry vinegar offers a musty, heady note to a dressing and is frequently used in Spanish dishes.

make life easy

what can be done in advance?

If it is simple to make salad, you will eat more of it. When making a dressing, double the quantity and have an extra jar in the fridge, the Sesame Ginger Soy and the Honey Mustard dressings (pages 18 and 19) keep well and instantly turn a bowl of vegetables into wonderful meals. Don't worry if olive oil turns to a solid in cold temperatures, let it come to room temperature before serving or stand the jar in hot water to melt it.

Many of the salads can be prepared in advance. The Hula Pork (page 74) is good for entertaining and so is the Pulled Lamb Shoulder with Date Crust (page 68) allowing you to prepare the accompanying dishes such as the Pineapple & Cashew Rice Salad (page 74) with a side of Roasted Peppers (page 74) and Guacamole (page 182) or the Tabbouleh (page 68) with a side of Jewelled Beetroot, Orange, Almond & Dill Salad (page 176)

cutting, chopping – what you will need

The food stylist on this book, Susie Theodorou, made our salads come to life. I thought I knew about chopping and cutting but it wasn't until she prepared the salads we photographed that I realised how ingredients could be cut so well and differently. Angles and sharp points on apple sticks, transparent veils of mandoline-cut celeriac and radish, using the whole vegetable and peppercorns crushed in a pestle and mortar made our salads look enticing and fresh.

If I had to choose three pieces of equipment, I would choose a sharp knife, a grater and a peeler. Ideally, sharpen your knife after chopping each onion – take out your sharpener and knife at the same time. A microplane grater is sharp and efficient, all graters become less sharp so admit this and don't struggle on with the same blunt one, replace as necessary. A potato peeler is good for creating shavings of vegetables as well as peeling them.

My next ideal pieces of equipment are a tomato knife, serrated and perfect for all soft-skinned fruits, and a julienne shredder – ours is from Vietnam and creates lengths of carrots and courgettes in no time. I also love our lime squeezer; it's not an essential, and a blast of 10 seconds in a microwave and a lemon squeezer is as good, but if you are squeezing a large quantity of limes, these are great. Mandolines need careful handling but are unbeatable if you want large thin slices.

Pinch off tough stems and tear herbs and salad leaves where possible unless the recipe calls for them to be finely cut. They will brown less quickly and retain their wild charm.

To peel a carrot or not to peel? It's a toss-up, many of the plant's nutrients lie just under the skin so by peeling the skin, you lose nutrition. However, dirt and pesticides are largely on the outside of the vegetable or fruit so peeling helps to rid them of chemicals. Eat clean where possible. Grow your own or buy organic if you can.

Above (left to right): a large handful of flat-leaf parsley; a small handful of flat-leaf parsley; stalks removed; 2 tablespoons of roughly chopped parsley; 1 heaped tablespoon of finely chopped parsley.

how to make the perfect salad

Through teaching in our cookery school we have developed a simple set of questions for students to ask themselves when preparing a dish, in this case a salad. After a while these guidelines become instinctive and help you create interesting and beautiful salads that everyone will enjoy:

- Do I have varying textures? Do I have something soft, chewy, crunchy, wet and dry?
- Would a little colour help? Do I need some berries, grated carrot, tomatoes or edible flowers from the garden?
- Should I add something creamy like a dip or pool of Greek yogurt or soured cream? (That will also fill you up and help the salad stick to the fork!)
- Do I have a balance of sweet and sour? Is my dressing too sweet or too acidic? Taste it and see, you would be amazed at how many people don't taste their food. Lemon will negate too much salt or sugar. Sugar alternatives like maple syrup will calm acid flavours.
- Can I taste everything or is one flavour out of balance? Keep bold with bold and subtle with subtle. Match the ingredients with the dressing. Delicate seafood might not appreciate too much spice and garlic. Kale will dominate a subtle dressing.
- Do I need a little mustard, garlic or chilli to give the salad some heat on a cold day or to fire up bland beans?
- Would a handful of herbs such as mint, parsley or coriander give the salad more zing?
- If the salad is a main meal, does it include protein, carbohydrate and fat to provide all the food groups?
- Seasoning, seasoning, seasoning. Apply salt and pepper to the cooked elements of a dish, onto salad leaves and into dressing. If you do this to taste you won't over-season. Use sea salt, fine or coarse, and always grind pepper in a mill or pestle and mortar, never buy the ready crushed stuff as the flavour will be long gone.
- Is the salad evenly dressed or are all the best bits at the top? Construct a salad in layers: ingredients, dressing, crunch, such as seeds or croutons, items that give bite, such as shavings of cheese, chilli or pickles, followed by another layer of leaves and so on. This way the last diner doesn't get a sad undressed pile of leaves.
- Finally, how does it look? I can't think of a savoury salad that is not better finished with a twist of black pepper.

serving salads

- Big bowls are essential for tossing salads.

- Dress salads at the last minute or they will wilt. Do this with your hands, gently giving the leaves a light coating rather than a drenching. Any extra dressing can be served on the side. At a buffet put the dressing in a jug to the side and let people do it themselves, the leaves will last longer.

- Use tongs to serve, you can operate them with one hand while holding a plate in the other. We have built up a collection of tongs: small green plastic, big metal ones, bamboo and wooden ones. I think they do the job much better than the traditional oversized spoon and fork.

- Individual salads look great and can be prepared in advance in champagne saucers, tumblers or even vintage teacups. Don't overfill them, so diners can toss the salad with the dressing served in shot glasses on the side.

- Ingredients don't have to be combined. I always remember the salad I saw a man eat in Italy. He had separate piles of anchovies, olives, mozzarella, tomato and cucumber, he loved them all but not together, preferring to eat his way around the plate, forming different combinations of flavours in every mouthful. The Poke Bowl (page 117) works well like this, as do the Japanese salads, like the Japanese Salmon Salad Bowl (pages 105–111), that are traditionally served in bento boxes.

- To transport a salad, pack the dressing separately or put it in the bottom of the jar, see page 142.

dressings

All the dressings can be made and shaken together (if necessary) in a lidded screw-top jar – that way they can be stored in the fridge in the same container without any need to cover them.

tahini citrus dressing

This tangy, nutty dressing has the consistency of mayonnaise and is perfect dolloped on salads with roasted vegetables, if you are using the salad in a jar idea (page 142), or with Falafel (page 146) or Chicken Shawarma (page 79). Or simply splash over roasted aubergine slices and top with fresh coriander.

makes 100ml/serves 6

3 tablespoons tahini
2 tablespoons extra virgin olive oil
1 medium garlic clove, finely grated
3 tablespoons orange juice
2 tablespoons lemon juice, plus extra to taste
¼–½ teaspoon finely grated lemon zest, to taste
salt and freshly ground black pepper

Mix the ingredients together in a small bowl or jar. Season to taste with extra lemon juice, salt and pepper if necessary. Use straight away or keep in the fridge for up to 3 days.

korean sesame yogurt sauce

This flavour-packed dressing is light and creamy and works brilliantly with mixed or green salads and on cold rice noodles. The recipe was given to me by a Korean lady in a nail bar in New Jersey who told me she loved it as yogurt made it a lighter dressing than those made with a lot of oil. She said you must include the ground and toasted sesame seeds – they are typical of Korean dressings and help emulsify the sauce.

makes 150ml/serves 6–8

4 tablespoons sesame seeds, toasted and ground
6 tablespoons natural yogurt
2 tablespoons extra virgin olive oil
1 teaspoon toasted sesame oil
2 teaspoons rice or white wine vinegar
2 teaspoons lemon juice, plus extra, to taste
2 teaspoons raw mild honey, plus extra, to taste
salt

Mix all the ingredients together in a small bowl or jug with 3 tablespoons of water. Season to taste with extra lemon juice, honey and salt. Use straight away or store for up to 5 days in the fridge.

sesame ginger soy dressing

This is our go-to Asian dressing and makes a perfect partner for salad, prawns, salmon or chicken. As chilli often features in Asian salads, none is included in this recipe. However, do add a little finely chopped chilli to taste if you prefer a dressing with more heat.

makes 150ml/serves 8–10

2 tablespoons flavourless oil, such as grapeseed, groundnut or olive
4 tablespoons lime juice or rice vinegar
3 tablespoons tamari or soy sauce
1–2 tablespoons raw mild honey, to taste
2 teaspoons grated fresh root ginger
1 teaspoon toasted sesame oil
1 garlic clove, finely grated
salt

Whisk the ingredients together in a small bowl or jug and season to taste. The dressing will keep in a lidded jar in the fridge for up to 3 days.

variation Add 1 tablespoon of crunchy or smooth peanut butter to the dressing.

nuoc cham vietnamese dipping sauce

We were introduced to this recipe by the energetic chef Duc Tran, who gives cookery courses and runs the Mango Rooms restaurant with his wife in Hoi An, Vietnam. Duc told us this versatile sauce is used for dipping, on salad or with grilled fish. He showed us how to mix it with coriander for another twist and pour it over grilled calamari or scallops on the half-shell. Use Vietnamese fish sauce if you can as it is more gentle than the Thai fish sauce, nam pla. If you leave it out, use a little salt instead.

makes approx. 80ml/serves 6–8

2 tablespoons lime juice (in Vietnam they use green small lemons or green kumquats)
2 tablespoons rice vinegar
2 teaspoons Vietnamese fish sauce
2 teaspoons raw mild honey
1 small garlic clove, finely chopped
1 red or green chilli, finely chopped
salt (optional)

Put the ingredients in a small bowl or jug and stir well to combine. Adjust the balance to taste with a little more fish sauce (or salt), honey or chilli.

Store in the fridge in a lidded jar for up to a week.

ponzu

Ponzu sauce is best known as the dipping sauce for Shabu Shabu, the Japanese beef dish. However, it is very versatile and great with seared tuna, grilled steak, fried aubergine slices, green or mixed salads and goes especially well with avocado.

Typically it is made with yuzu juice, a Japanese citrus fruit with a sour grapefruit flavour which gives it a bright citrus zing. The fruit is almost impossible to find in Europe but it is available as a juice from specialist stores, some supermarkets and online. Make sure you choose pure juice, though, not a yuzu dressing which has other flavours added. If you can't get hold of it, use a mixture of lemon, lime and grapefruit juice.

This recipe is from Atsuko, who teaches Japanese cookery classes in London. She is married to an Italian man and knows how to cook Japanese food for Europeans. She has simplified this Ponzu recipe to make it easy to whip up and enjoy at home.

makes 150ml/serves 8–10

3 tablespoons rice vinegar
3 tablespoons light soy sauce
3 tablespoons mirin or sweet white wine
½ teaspoon salt
½–1 teaspoon raw mild honey
2 tablespoons yuzu juice or a mixture of lemon, lime and grapefruit juice

Mix the ingredients together in a bowl, stirring well to dissolve the honey. Season to taste with yuzu juice, salt and honey. Store in the fridge for up to 3 days.

honey mustard dressing

This utterly moreish, creamy dressing has a fiery kick from the French and English mustards. It is delicious tossed with hot new potatoes and parsley, over hot vegetables, on leaf salads, or those with chicken or ham.

makes 150ml/serves 10–12

2 tablespoons smooth or wholegrain Dijon mustard
2 teaspoons English mustard
2 teaspoons raw mild honey or maple syrup, plus extra to taste
2 tablespoons lemon juice or cider or wine vinegar
8 tablespoons extra virgin olive oil
salt and freshly ground black pepper

Whisk together the mustards, honey or syrup, lemon juice or vinegar with a little salt and pepper. Slowly add the oil and continue to whisk until emulsified. Add extra honey or syrup to taste. Enjoy straight away or store in the fridge for up 2 weeks. Bring to room temperature before use.

classic vinaigrette

I am convinced it is this dressing that got me hooked on cooking at an early age. My mother would ask me to taste the dressing and tell her if it needed more acidity or sweetness. My young palate was trained and she empowered me with a sense that my opinion counted. Always taste the dressing before using, it varies according to the strength of vinegar and your own taste buds.

**serves 6–8/
makes approx. 100ml**

2 tablespoons red wine vinegar

8 tablespoons extra virgin olive oil, plus
    extra, to taste

1–2 teaspoons raw mild honey or maple
    syrup, to taste

2 teaspoons Dijon mustard

1 medium garlic clove, finely chopped

salt and freshly ground black pepper

Put the ingredients into a lidded jar and shake to combine. Taste and add more oil and honey or syrup, if necessary.

Stored in a lidded jar, in the fridge, for up to a week. Remove from the fridge 30 minutes before you need it and shake before serving.

Variations

Balsamic Use a good-quality balsamic instead of red wine vinegar.

Malt vinegar Very popular in Australia, it gives a malty tang.

Herb Add 2 tablespoons chopped leafy herbs such as basil, coriander, chives or parsley.

Nut Swap half the olive oil for walnut or hazelnut oil.

Creamy Reduce the oil by half and make up with crème fraîche or double cream.

Fruit Use a fruit-flavoured vinegar, such as raspberry or blackberry, but taste before adding the sugar or syrup as fruit vinegars are usually sweet.

caesar's salad dressing

To make the sauce for Caesar salad we followed the suggestion in *Roberta's Cookbook*, of using roasted garlic for a wonderfully mellow flavour. You will have more roasted garlic than you need but the rest can be stirred into salad dressings or spread on hot toast. We also tried smoked garlic, which was lovely, too.

makes approx. 220ml/ serves 8–10

1 whole garlic bulb
2 tablespoons olive oil
1 garlic clove, roughly chopped
1 teaspoon lemon juice, plus extra to taste
4 anchovy fillets under oil, drained, plus extra to taste
1 quantity of Mayonnaise with Dijon mustard (see right)
freshly ground black pepper

Preheat the oven to 180°C/gas mark 4. Cut 5mm off the pointed end of the bulb of garlic and put it, cut-side up, on a square of foil. Drizzle over the olive oil, add a splash of water and bring the corners of the foil up around the garlic and twist to secure so that it steams inside a loose foil package. Place on a baking tray and bake for 45 minutes– 1 hour or until the garlic is soft to the touch. Remove and leave to cool in the foil.

Squeeze out 3 medium garlic cloves from the roasted bulb and squash into a paste, using the flat side of a knife or a small blender, with the raw garlic, lemon juice, anchovies and a twist of black pepper.

Stir the mixture into the mayonnaise and add more roasted garlic, lemon juice and anchovies according to your liking.

Transfer to an airtight lidded container and store in the fridge for up to 7 days.

mayonnaise

This is chef Stefano Borella's mayonnaise. Stefano is the main teacher at our cookery school and since our son Flavio is rather addicted to the shop-bought variety I sent him to Stefano to find out what real mayonnaise tastes like! Lemon juice or vinegar work equally well but do give slightly different flavours. Mustard and garlic are added for taste only. It is fun to experiment with reasonably small quantities such as this to achieve a perfectly flavoured mayonnaise. The same is true for oils, we prefer a neutral-flavoured oil, such as groundnut or grapeseed, rather than rapeseed or olive oil, but a small amount of extra virgin olive oil added at the end can give a subtle difference.

Our favourite concoction is groundnut oil with extra virgin oil, white wine vinegar, Dijon mustard and no garlic.

makes approx. 220ml/ serves 8–10

3 free-range egg yolks
½ teaspoon fine salt
2 tablespoons white wine vinegar or lemon juice, plus extra to taste
150ml groundnut or lightly flavoured seed oil or 125ml nut or seed oil and 25ml extra virgin olive oil
2 teaspoons English or Dijon mustard (optional)
1 garlic clove, finely chopped (optional)

If making mayonnaise by hand, put a damp cloth under a bowl and use a balloon whisk. Alternatively use a blender – we like to use an electric whisk with one beater attached.

Put the egg yolks, salt and vinegar or lemon juice into the bowl. Whisk together until smooth. Slowly add a thin stream of oil, continuing to whisk until it is thick and all the oil is used.

Add the mustard and garlic, if using, and continue to whisk. Taste and add a little more lemon juice or vinegar and salt, if necessary. Adjust the density by whisking in a little warm water if it is too thick. Use straight away or store in the fridge in an airtight container for up to 7 days.

Variations

Chipotle Mayonnaise Stir together 100ml mayonnaise, 50ml soured cream, 1 teaspoon chipotle smoked chilli paste or powder and 1 tablespoon lime juice.

Lemon Mayonnaise Use lemon juice instead of vinegar and add a little finely grated lemon zest to taste.

Aïoli Add 2 crushed garlic cloves to the mix at the end, fold in and let it stand for a few hours to develop the flavour.

Saffron Mayonnaise Infuse ½ teaspoon of saffron strands in a tablespoon of very hot water for a few minutes until cool and add the liquid and the strands at the end of mixing the mayonnaise.

rise & shine

watermelon & feta salad with mint vinaigrette

smoked whitefish salad

sugar snap salad & pea pancakes with peppered mackerel

spinach, bacon, avocado & tomato salad with poached eggs

swedish cucumber salad

saffron peach & mint salad with banana pancakes & lemon crème fraîche

ginger & turmeric fruit salad with whipped coconut cream

overnight bircher & berry salad

watermelon & feta salad with mint vinaigrette

serves 4–6

This is a recipe from our Egyptian chef friend Moustafa el Refaey. We love the combination of feta and sweet ripe watermelon but Moustafa makes it even better with this luscious minty dressing. It makes a refreshing breakfast, starter or a light dessert.

for the dressing
8g mint leaves (no thick stems)
2 tablespoons white wine vinegar
60ml extra virgin olive oil
1 teaspoon raw mild honey
salt and freshly ground black pepper

for the salad
500g watermelon flesh, deseeded and cut into 3cm cubes
200g feta cheese, cut into rough 1 x 3cm rectangles
150g cucumber, peeled and cut into 1cm cubes
a few small mint leaves, to garnish

Whizz the dressing ingredients together in a blender until smooth, it will be flecked with green. Mix the melon, cheese and cucumber gently together with the dressing. Enjoy straight away or keep in the fridge for up to 4 hours. Serve in chilled glasses or bowls and garnish with the mint leaves.

smoked whitefish salad

serves 4

There is a long history in New York of the Jewish delicacy of smoked fish known simply as 'whitefish'. Russ & Daughters, the wonderful hundred-year-old Jewish deli, is well known for it and the more recent arrival, Mile End Deli, serves whitefish salad, which inspired this recipe.

We like it with poached eggs on buttered sourdough toast or rye bagels for weekend brunches. Dollops of creamy homemade mayo, or Lemon Mayonnaise (page 21) served on the side, help the salad stick to the toast.

250g undyed smoked haddock, cod or other flaky white fish
2 celery sticks, finely cut on the diagonal, and leaves, roughly torn
2 spring onions, finely cut on the diagonal
a small handful of flat-leaf or curly parsley
a few sprigs of dill
juice of ½ lemon
2 tablespoons extra virgin olive oil
salt and freshly ground black pepper

to serve (optional)
homemade Mayonnaise (page 21)
poached eggs
buttered toast or bagels

Poach the fish in simmering water until cooked through. Depending on the thickness it will take 5–10 minutes. Remove any bones and skin. Drain and leave to cool.

Flake the fish onto a large plate. Top with the celery, celery leaves and onions. Tear the parsley leaves from the stems over the salad. Pick off the little fronds of dill and scatter them over. Mix the lemon juice, oil and seasoning in a small bowl or jug and pour evenly over the salad.

Serve the salad as it is (for a gluten and dairy-free option) or with mayonnaise, poached eggs and buttered toast or bagels.

sugar snap salad & pea pancakes with peppered mackerel

serves 4–6

These little green blini-style pancakes stack neatly in the middle of a board and everyone reaches in to grab one. We spread them with dill crème fraîche and add our choice of smoked mackerel, smoked salmon or trout. A perfect weekend breakfast or a light lunch with the salad.

The dill crème fraîche needs to develop over a few hours so do try to make in advance, at least 3 hours is good and once made it lasts for up to 4 days in the fridge. Reiko's Pickled Cucumbers (page 110) are another great accompaniment.

for the dill crème fraîche

200ml crème fraîche

3 heaped tablespoons finely chopped dill

1–2 teaspoons raw mild honey

1 teaspoon Dijon mustard

1 tablespoon lemon juice

salt and freshly ground black pepper

for the pancakes

300g frozen or fresh peas

a small handful of mint leaves

3 spring onions, roughly chopped

50g buckwheat or plain flour

2 eggs

3–4 tablespoons groundnut or grapeseed oil

1–2 tablespoons almond or cow's milk (optional)

for the salad

200g sugar snap peas, mangetout or French beans

3 spring onions, cut into 3cm diagonal slices

200g baby courgettes, shaved into ribbons

2 Little Gem lettuces

a handful of pink radishes, finely sliced

a small bunch of dill, torn into small fronds

a handful of mint leaves

4 tablespoons extra virgin olive oil

1 tablespoon lemon juice

for the fish

3 peppered smoked mackerel or 200g smoked salmon or trout

 If using buckwheat flour for the pancakes.

First make the dill crème fraîche by mixing the ingredients together, taste and adjust the seasoning as necessary. Decant into a bowl and set aside in the fridge.

To make the pancakes, cook the peas until just tender. This will take 3–4 minutes from frozen or up to 15 minutes if fresh. Drain and pour into ice-cold water to cool them down quickly. When cool, drain and pour into a food processor with the remaining pancake ingredients, apart from the milk. Whizz until smooth and add 1–2 tablespoons of milk, if necessary, until you have a dropping consistency (you may not need any). Set aside while you make the salad.

Boil the sugar snap peas until just tender, about 3 minutes should do it. Drain and put into ice-cold water to cool, keep their colour and stop the cooking. Toss the remaining salad ingredients in a bowl, season to taste and set aside.

To make the pancakes, heat a little oil in a large non-stick frying pan. Add a dollop of pea batter and let it spread a little. The pancakes can be small like blinis or larger like drop scones, as you wish. Fry for a couple of minutes on either side, flipping them over halfway through cooking. They should be browned on both sides and cooked through. Taste the first one to check the seasoning before cooking any more. Repeat to use up all the batter to make about 20 blini-size pancakes. The pancakes can be served at room temperature or kept warm in a low oven (about 50°C).

Now assemble the salad on a large platter or wooden board with the pancakes, bowl of crème fraîche, fish broken up a little and put into a pile.

variation

For a vegetarian option use 200g crumbled feta cheese instead of the fish.

spinach, bacon, avocado & tomato salad with poached eggs

serves 4

The alluring aroma of bacon rashers crisping in the pan is the best alarm call I can give our teenage boys. This is a nutritious and satisfying breakfast that sets us up for the day. Later in the day, for lunch or dinner, I serve this with crumbled chorizo instead; I find the strong garlic flavour a little too much first thing. If you have a good avocado oil in the house, this is the time to use it.

6 rashers of smoked streaky bacon, roughly chopped or 1 chorizo sausage, crumbled

1 large Hass avocado, sliced

a large handful of spinach leaves or beetroot leaves or watercress

150g cherry or medium tomatoes, quartered

a good squeeze of lemon juice

2 tablespoons avocado oil or extra virgin olive oil

4 eggs

salt and freshly ground black pepper

4 slices buttered sourdough toast, to serve (optional)

  If serving without toast.

Cook the bacon or chorizo in a small frying pan until cooked through and slightly crisp. Set aside on kitchen paper to drain. Put it in a bowl with the avocado, leaves, tomatoes, lemon juice, oil and seasoning. Toss to combine.

To soft-poach the eggs, bring a medium saucepan of water to a gentle boil. Crack the eggs, one at a time, into a cup. Create a whirlpool in the water by whirring a fork round and round in it. Gently pour in the egg. Do one at a time. Keep the heat high but not so high that the foam boils over. Scoop out any unattached egg-white strands. Boil for 3 minutes or until the egg white is opaque. Lift out with a slotted spoon when ready and drain on kitchen paper. Repeat with the remaining eggs.

Serve the eggs, on toast if you wish, with the salad alongside.

swedish cucumber salad

serves 6–8

We made a salad like this in our book *The Gentle Art of Preserving*, which preserved cucumbers through the winter by adding salt and vinegar. As the cucumbers are cut thinly here the effect is similar but much quicker, giving a crunchy fresh-tasting salad. It's great served with smoked or salt-cured salmon, the Hot Pink Beetroot & Apple Salad (page 153) or the Sugar Snap Salad & Pea Pancakes with Peppered Mackerel (page 28). This dish is best with small cucumbers, that have few seeds, if you can find them.

4 small cucumbers or 1 English long cucumber

1 teaspoon salt

1 shallot, thinly sliced

1 tablespoon finely chopped dill

1 tablespoon finely chopped flat-leaf or curly parsley

2 tablespoons cider vinegar

1 tablespoon raw mild honey

Cut some of the skin of the cucumbers away lengthways to create long thick or thin stripes. This can be done with a specially designed cutting tool or potato peeler. Cut the cucumbers in half lengthways and use a teaspoon to scrape out the seeds. Next lay the cucumber halves down onto a board and cut into half-moon shapes, about 2mm wide. Mix them in a bowl with the salt and then transfer to a sieve to drain for 30 minutes.

Gently press the cucumbers into the sieve with a large spoon to rid them of any remaining water. Mix with the remaining ingredients in a bowl. Taste and adjust the seasoning as necessary. Toss to combine and serve straight away or store, in a covered container, for up to 3 days in the fridge.

saffron peach & mint salad with banana pancakes & lemon crème fraîche

serves 6

These perfumed peaches are another great recipe from Moustafa, our Egyptian chef friend in Cairo. They are particularly good with a spray of rose water over the top. If you are being super healthy omit the sugar and butter from the peaches if you prefer, they brown well under the grill if left naked but can be a little dry. As saffron is an acquired taste, I normally do a few plain buttered peaches and some with saffron strands.

We love to have this for a weekend breakfast with coffee but the peaches would work equally well without the pancakes as a dessert.

for the granola
Use the ingredients for the stuffing for the Roast Figs & Apricots (page 202)

for the lemon crème fraîche
200ml crème fraîche
finely grated zest of ½ lemon
1 teaspoon lemon juice
1 teaspoon raw mild honey or caster sugar, plus extra to taste

for the pancakes
2 ripe bananas
3 eggs
50g oats
2 tablespoons flaxseed
1 vanilla pod, seeds only or ½ teaspoon vanilla extract
2 tablespoons groundnut oil or spray oil, for frying

for the peaches
6 peaches
15g butter, melted
½ teaspoon saffron strands (optional)
1 tablespoon raw mild honey

to serve
raw mild honey
rose water
mint leaves

Preheat the oven to 130°C/gas mark 1 and line a baking tray with baking parchment.

To make the granola, whizz the dates, sultanas, dried apples, vanilla extract, cinnamon and nuts in a food processor until they form a rough paste. Remove from the processor and stir in the pumpkin seeds. Use your hands to bring the mixture into a ball and then crumble into small pieces and spread out onto the lined tray. Bake for 15–20 minutes or until firm to the touch, dry through to the centre and crunchy. Leave to cool and transfer to an airtight container – they will keep for up to 5 days.

Meanwhile, mix the lemon crème fraîche ingredients together, taste and add extra honey or sugar if necessary. Decant into a bowl and set aside in the fridge until needed. It will keep for up to 3 days.

To make the pancakes, whizz the ingredients together in a blender until smooth. Heat the oil in a large non-stick frying pan and when hot pour in a tablespoon of the mixture, spread it out a little with a heatproof spatula or palette knife to about 10cm. You can cook 2–3 pancakes depending on the size of your pan. When cooked on one side and the batter is set, flip to the other side with the spatula. Continue to cook until the pancakes are lightly golden and cooked through. Keep hot in the still-warm oven while you cook the remaining batter – you should have 16–18 pancakes in total.

Preheat the grill to high. Cut the peaches in half and remove the stones by hand or with a sharp knife. Brush on the butter, mixed with the saffron, if using, and drizzle over the honey. Grill the peaches cut-side up for about 15 minutes or until they start to brown.

To serve, crumble the granola bites over the peaches and place on the banana pancakes, add a dollop of lemon crème fraîche, a drizzle of honey and a spritz of rose water, if you like it, and a few mint leaves.

ginger & turmeric fruit salad with whipped coconut cream

serves 4

This is based on our friend Sally Dorling's recipe for a healthy breakfast or dessert salad. She serves this with ginger yogurt, which is a lovely and instant pairing. Our twist is to add turmeric, which lends it a golden orange glow as well as a string of potential health benefits. Turmeric is good for any inflammation and ginger settles the stomach. We love it too with with coconut cream, which lowers the spike of insulin in your blood sugar that normally occurs when you eat fruit.

for the whipped coconut cream

400ml can coconut milk

2 teaspoons raw mild honey or maple syrup (for a vegan option),
    plus extra to taste

1 teaspoon vanilla extract

for the fruit salad

500g fruits, such as melon, mango, pineapple, lychees,
    grapes, apples

2 teaspoons finely grated fresh turmeric or 1 teaspoon
    dried turmeric powder

2 teaspoons finely grated fresh root ginger

juice of 1 orange

      If using maple syrup.

Put the can of coconut cream in the fridge for at least 3 hours to set. Scoop off the solid cream (about 130–150g) from the top and transfer to a bowl. Reserve the remaining liquid for another use, such as in a smoothie (I use it in coffee). Use a hand whisk or electric mixer to whip the coconut into firm peaks. Add the honey or maple syrup and vanilla to taste. Store in an airtight lidded container in the fridge for up to 3 days.

Peel and cut the fruits into bite-sized pieces and put in a serving bowl. Add the grated roots to the orange juice and mix well. Pour over the cut fruit and toss to combine. Serve straight away or chill in the fridge overnight until ready to serve.

Serve the fruits with the whipped coconut cream.

overnight bircher
& berry salad

serves 4

This is a healthy version of a basic bircher muesli topped with fruit salad. You can adapt it by adding a variety of seeds and nuts including chia seeds, flaxseed, sunflower seeds, walnuts or almonds. When fresh berries aren't in season, serve the muesli with dried fruits such as apricots and prunes, dates, soaked goji berries, bananas or coconut flakes. The bircher can also be served topped with natural or coconut yogurt and bee pollen. I find it sweet enough, but do add honey or maple syrup for those with a sweet tooth.

100g oats

150ml unsweetened almond, coconut or cow's milk or water

juice of 1 orange

50g whole skin-on almonds

1 apple, cored and coarsely grated

1 tablespoons seeds, such as chia, sunflower or pumpkin

1–2 tablespoons raw mild honey or maple syrup for a vegan option (optional)

½ teaspoon ground cinnamon (optional)

125g mixed berries, such as strawberries, blackberries, blueberries and raspberries

   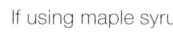 If using maple syrup.

Soak the oats in a bowl with the milk and juice in the fridge overnight. Soak the almonds in another bowl covered in water in the fridge. The following day drain the almonds and roughly chop. Add them and the apple, seeds, honey and ground cinnamon, if using, and stir into the mixture. If at this point the mixture is a little too thick, add a splash more milk to loosen it. Spoon into glasses and top with the berries. Eat straight away or store in the fridge overnight to eat the following day.

2

first things first

green juice salad

vietnamese vegetables with dipping sauces

fig, nectarine, burrata & prosciutto salad with honey dressing

whole lettuce salad with gorgonzola dolce & hot bacon vinaigrette

romaine caesar salad with candied walnuts

avocado & rocket salad with balsamic strawberry & basil cashew dressing

roast cauliflower in garam masala with mango yogurt dressing

korean grapefruit & strawberry salad

italian seafood salad

chargrilled squid, potato, watercress with green breadcrumbs & lemon dressing

thai poached prawn, carrot & coriander salad

vietnamese spring rolls

beetroot & salmon tiradito

simple sea bream, grape & celery ceviche

sea bass, lime & coriander ceviche

the dip of joy

shaved manchego, celeriac & radish salad with white truffle oil

endive, piquillo pepper & chorizo salad

green juice salad

serves 4

This unusual first course is based on Ignacio Mattos' Burrata with Salsa Verde at his incredible restaurant in New York, Estela, where he serves a whole ripe burrata in a green sea of spicy sorrel juice. If you can find sorrel use it in combination with spinach, otherwise spinach is a good alternative.

I like to serve this before a meal or after a main course in vintage Champagne saucers, as it is so refreshing. It is also good for breakfast on a sunny day, in which case, I leave out the garlic.

for the juice

50g sorrel and 50g spinach or 100g spinach

½ medium ripe, but not soft, pear, peeled and cored

100g celery sticks

½ medium garlic clove

a few slices of hot green chilli, to taste

10g fresh root ginger, peeled and roughly chopped

pinch of salt

for the salad

1 courgette, cut into 1cm dice

½ English cucumber, peeled, deseeded and cut into 1cm dice

125g ball buffalo mozzarella, torn into 8 pieces

1 medium avocado, cut into 1cm dice

Prepare the salad first. Put the diced courgette and cucumber into a bowl and place in the fridge to chill. Put the mozzarella into a sieve to drain and keep in the fridge. (The avocado should be cut just before serving or it will brown.) Put the juice ingredients, with 200ml cold water, in a blender and whizz until smooth. Strain through a fine sieve. Taste and adjust the flavour accordingly. It should be strong with a little spice and heat. Keep chilled until you are ready to serve. The juice will keep for up to 1 day in the fridge.

Pour the juice into individual glasses or one large bowl and add the vegetables and cheese just before serving.

vietnamese vegetables with dipping sauces

serves 6

Sticks of vegetables such as green and yellow courgette, carrots and red pepper are perfect for dipping into coriander chutney and peanut dipping sauce. We saw this done at the wonderful vegetarian restaurant Hum, in Saigon. This is brilliant for entertaining or for a healthy snack for kids and it is also a great way to use up gluts of courgette and limp coriander that would otherwise be thrown away.

for the peanut dipping sauce

120g crunchy peanut butter

1 tablespoon tamarind sauce or extra lime or lemon juice

1 tablespoon soy sauce

2 tablespoons lime or lemon juice

¼–½ red or green hot chilli, finely chopped (optional)

1–2 teaspoons raw mild honey, according to taste

salt, according to taste

for the coriander chutney

1 huge bunch, about 200g, of fresh coriander

100g roasted, skinned cashews or peanuts

4 tablespoons lemon juice

½–1 teaspoon salt

1 teaspoon raw mild honey (optional)

½–1 green chilli, deseeded and roughly chopped, adding
according to strength

15g fresh root ginger, peeled and roughly chopped

for the vegetables

2 red peppers

2 medium green or yellow courgettes

2 medium carrots

Put the ingredients for the peanut dipping sauce in a bowl with 75ml cold water and stir well to combine. Adjust the seasoning to taste. Store in a jar in the fridge for up to 4 days.

Put the ingredients for the coriander chutney in a food processor and whizz until blended, adding up to 100ml cold water to form a smooth, spreadable dip. Store in a jar in the fridge for up to 4 days.

Trim and prepare the vegetables and cut them into bite-sized batons. Serve with the dips on the side.

fig, nectarine, burrata & prosciutto salad with honey dressing

serves 6

This modern classic is lovely with burrata or mozzarella, drizzled with honey and oil. Spend on ingredients, not on time, and appreciate the simple pleasures in life; splash out on a creamy burrata, the best tomatoes you can find and a really good single estate olive oil. Use seasonal sweet summer fruits such as figs or cherries – the important thing is that they are ripe and flavourful.

for the honey dressing

1 tablespoon raw mild honey

2 tablespoons good-quality olive oil

salt and freshly ground black pepper

for the salad

6 ripe figs, torn in half or quarters depending on size

2 nectarines, sliced thinly

6 x 125g whole burrata or mozzarella

12 slices of prosciutto

200g cherry tomatoes, halved

12 large basil leaves

Mix the ingredients for the dressing together in a small bowl or jug and season lightly, to taste, remembering the cheese and ham are slightly salty, too.

Arrange the salad ingredients on a serving platter and pour over the honey dressing.

whole lettuce salad with gorgonzola dolce & hot bacon vinaigrette

serves 6

Stefano Borella, chef at our cookery school, comes from the Italian mountains. When his family's supply of olive oil ran out his grandmother would use hot pork fat and homemade vinegar to dress salad. We thought that sounded lovely so we experimented with using the fat in the pan after cooking bacon.

This is the result – an indulgent, heavenly heap of salad, smoky bacon and soft cheese. Serve it on a big board while still warm and let everyone pull off a leaf. The lettuce and dressing can be prepared in advance and assembled at the last moment.

The lettuce is important here, it should be the soft leaves of a Butterhead or Boston lettuce – round, floppy leaves with a mild flavour. Little Gem leaves can also work if pulled apart and filled as individual servings, but cut away any bitter stalks.

1 round, soft-leaved lettuce

250g fatty, streaky, smoked bacon rashers, cut into 1cm strips

100ml extra virgin olive oil

25g pine nuts, split almonds or hazelnuts

200g Gorgonzola Dolce

2 tablespoons red wine vinegar

salt and freshly ground black pepper

Wash and dry the whole lettuce, then leave to drain upside down on kitchen paper to gather the last drips of water. The bitter, chunky stem should be trimmed, allowing the flower shape to open, but do try to keep it just intact at the base.

Fry the bacon in a large non-stick frying pan over a low heat in the olive oil until just crisp. The oil then forms dressing.

Dry-fry the nuts in a non-stick frying pan over a medium heat for 5–7 minutes until lightly browned.

Meanwhile, put the lettuce onto a board or large serving plate and gently open up the leaves like the petals of a flower. Using your fingers, tear off pieces of the cheese (it's messy but the most efficient way to do this; the cheese is just too soft and sticky for spoons) and put a bite-sized piece into each leaf.

Add the vinegar to the bacon and oil in the pan and plenty of black pepper. Add a little salt to taste but if the bacon is salty you may not need any.

To serve, pour the dressing and bacon evenly over the lettuce and scatter over the nuts. Provide napkins as this is best eaten with your fingers, straight from the board, folding up the lettuce leaves around the cheese, bacon and dressing.

romaine caesar salad with candied walnuts

serves 6

I wasn't going to include Caesar salad here as recipes abound in books and online. However, when I tasted the light, tangy roasted garlic mayonnaise that coated the crisp whole leaves of romaine at Roberta's restaurant, in Brooklyn, I changed my mind and have only made a few changes to their brilliant recipe. If you have any dressing leftover it's wonderful on potatoes or eggs.

The salad is layered with candied nuts – softer nuts such as walnuts and pecans are ideal for candying. They also make an irresistible snack or topping for many other salads.

for the candied nuts

400g walnuts or pecans or a mixture

2 egg whites

30g dark brown sugar

75g raw mild honey or maple syrup

½ teaspoon freshly ground black pepper

1 teaspoon salt

for the salad

2 Romaine lettuces, trimmed and leaves separated

1 quantity of Aïoli (page 21)

100g Parmigiano Reggiano or mature Pecorino cheese

freshly ground black pepper

Preheat the oven to 180°C/gas mark 4. Line a baking tray with baking parchment.

Put the nuts on the lined tray and roast for 12 minutes, turning the tray once during this time to ensure even cooking. Remove from the oven and leave to cool to room temperature. Reduce the oven temperature to 130°C/gas mark 1.

In a large mixing bowl, whisk the egg whites to the stage just before they form peaks when you lift the whisk out. Add the sugar, honey and black pepper and whisk again to combine.

Pour the nuts from the paper into the bowl and use a large spoon to stir them so that all are coated in the sticky mixture. Now use a slotted spoon to scoop them up and spread them out onto the baking tray lined with baking parchment again. Scatter over the salt evenly with your fingers and bake the nuts for 25 minutes, turning the tray halfway through. The nuts should be dry and not sticky to the touch, if they are then bake for a few minutes longer but don't let them burn. Remove from the oven and leave to cool, then store in an airtight container for up to 2 weeks.

To assemble the salad, wash and dry the lettuce. Put a few lettuce leaves into a large serving bowl and drizzle over a little dressing. I use a leaf to spread it out, then grate over a thin layer of cheese, scatter over a few nuts and give it a grind of pepper. Repeat the layering, until you finish the leaves, saving any leftover dressing and nuts for another day.

avocado & rocket salad with balsamic strawberry & basil cashew dressing

serves 4–6

Vegan chef Sara Mittersteiner gave me this recipe for one of her favourite salads. Sara is from Parma so she knows her balsamic vinegars and always chooses one made in the traditional way in Modena. Nutritional yeast is included to impart a savoury flavour and valuable B12 vitamin. If you can't find it, leave it out, the dressing is delicious just the same.

for the dressing
50g soaked cashews (see page 13)
2 tablespoons tapioca flour
1 tablespoon extra virgin olive oil
2 tablespoons balsamic vinegar
1 small garlic clove
1 tablespoon nutritional yeast (optional)
½ teaspoon salt
1 tablespoon lime juice
5 basil leaves
125g strawberries
½ teaspoon pink peppercorns

for the salad
100g rocket leaves
1 large avocado, sliced
2 tablespoons dried cranberries, halved if big
100g canned lychees, drained and quartered
extra virgin olive oil, for drizzling
a few pink peppercorns, to garnish

Put the dressing ingredients in a blender, with 2 tablespoons of cold water, and whizz until very smooth and silky.

Arrange the salad ingredients on serving plates and drizzle with a little extra virgin olive oil.

Serve the dressing separately or pour a little onto each salad. Garnish with a few pink peppercorns, crushing them between your fingers as they fall.

roast cauliflower in garam masala with mango yogurt dressing

serves 4–6

This is easy, quick and no one will know you haven't slaved over a hot pot of chutney to whistle up this appetiser or side dish. Cauliflowers are cheap, but do invest in a good-quality mango chutney (we like Geeta's, the one with black onion seeds in) for great flavour. Dip the florets into the sauce and then into the nuts to eat.

for the cauliflower
500g cauliflower, cut into walnut-sized florets and any leaves, cut
    into batons
5 tablespoons groundnut or seed oil
1 tablespoon garam masala
1 teaspoon ground cumin
2 garlic cloves, finely chopped
salt and freshly ground black pepper

for the mango dipping sauce
100g mango chutney
50g thick natural yogurt
a few black onion seeds
75g toasted whole (skin-on) or flaked almonds, to serve
roughly chopped coriander leaves, to garnish

Preheat the oven to 180°C/gas mark 4. Put the florets into a large bowl and toss with the oil, spices, garlic and seasoning to coat. Spread them out on a baking tray and roast for about 30 minutes or until just browned and at the point when they start to soften.

Meanwhile, for the dipping sauce, if the chutney has pieces in it, whizz in a food processor first or finely chop the pieces by hand. Mix the chutney and yogurt together. Spoon into a small serving dish and scatter over the black onion seeds. Break up the nuts a little with a sharp knife and put into another small dish.

Arrange the cauliflower on a serving plate garnished with the coriander leaves and the bowls of dip and nuts.

korean grapefruit & strawberry salad

serves 4

Hangawi, a vegetarian Korean restaurant run by Terri Choi, is an oasis of taste and charm bang in the centre of New York. The grapefruit in the salad was inspired and gave it a sweet and sour flavour. My sister and I also loved the crunchy avocado bites with their luscious creamy insides. They were served on another salad but we loved them so much I have added them here.

Terri introduced me to liquid amino acids. They can be bought in a bottle easily online or in health food shops as a healthy alternative to soy sauce. Do seek out a bottle, the flavour is like nothing else, fruity, savoury and completely lovely.

We like this salad as a light starter for a dinner party. The salad ingredients can be prepared and left in the fridge, and the fresh avocado and rocket added at the last minute. The avocado bites can be reheated briefly in the oven after being fried and cooled. Simply pour the dressing on just before serving and top with warm avocado bites.

for the dressing

2 teaspoons rice vinegar, plus extra to taste

2 tablespoons (untoasted) sesame, groundnut or grapeseed oil

2 tablespoon liquid amino acids or light soy sauce,
    plus extra to taste

2 teaspoons toasted sesame seeds, ground

1 teaspoon raw mild honey or maple syrup (for a vegan option),
    plus extra to taste

for the crispy avocado bites

1 firm, ripe avocado, peeled, stoned and cut into 1.5cm cubes

50g plain or rice flour, for coating

100ml sparkling water

250ml groundnut or seed oil, for frying

for the salad

1 pink grapefruit

8 strawberries, hulled and sliced

1 large carrot, peeled into thin ribbons

1 avocado, peeled, stoned and cut into bite-sized pieces

a handful of rocket leaves

2 spring onions, finely chopped

1 tablespoon toasted sesame seeds

    If using maple syrup.

Peel and cut the grapefruit into segments and halve each. Catch any juices and add them to the dressing ingredients in a bowl. Whisk together and taste. Adjust the seasoning and balance as necessary.

Whisk together the flour with the sparkling water. Heat the oil over a high heat in a small high-sided saucepan until a small piece of bread sizzles in the oil. Dip the avocado cubes into the batter. Increase the heat to medium–high and fry the avocado for 3–5 minutes in the hot oil or until lightly browned. Drain on kitchen paper and scatter with a little salt. If they become cold reheat in the oven briefly.

Divide the salad ingredients between four serving dishes. Pour over the dressing and top with the hot avocado bites and sesame seeds.

italian seafood salad

serves 6–8

To enjoy this colourful and flavoursome salad at its best, make it the day before you want to eat, to allow the seafood to soak in the Mediterranean flavours. Serve with plenty of bread to mop up the dressing or stir into cooked and cooled rice.

500g white fish fillets, such as sea bass or bream

500g mixed seafood, including peeled prawns, scallops and squid

½–1 red chilli, finely sliced, according to taste

a handful of green or black olives, halved and pitted

1 garlic clove, finely chopped

2 tablespoons white wine vinegar

2 tablespoons lemon juice, plus extra to taste

150ml extra virgin olive oil

1 medium carrot, finely shredded

½ red pepper, thinly sliced into batons

4 large or 8 small sun-dried tomatoes, thinly sliced (optional)

1 celery stick, finely cut into julienne strips

a few fresh oregano leaves or ½ teaspoon dried oregano

salt and freshly ground black pepper

chopped flat-leaf parsley, to garnish

crusty bread, to serve (optional)

Cook the fish fillets in lightly salted boiling water for 2–4 minutes until just cooked. Remove from the water with a fish slice and set aside to cool. Peel away the skin and roughly break up the flesh into bite-sized pieces. If not using pre-prepared seafood, clean the squid and cut into 1cm pieces. Then cook the seafood in the same water for 2–4 minutes or until they are just cooked through. The prawns will turn pink when they are cooked. Drain and set aside to cool.

Put all the remaining ingredients, except the parsley, in a bowl. Gently toss to combine taking care not to break up the fish. Cover and marinate overnight in the fridge. The following day adjust the seasoning to taste with salt, pepper and lemon juice. Serve garnished with parsley with some crusty bread, if you like. The salad will keep, in a lidded airtight container, for up to 3 days in the fridge.

chargrilled squid, potato, watercress with green breadcrumbs & lemon dressing

serves 6

Soft squid and crumbly potatoes are set off perfectly here with crunchy herb breadcrumbs and citrus dressing. Enjoy this salad as a light lunch or starter. We learnt to make these green breadcrumbs in Sicily, where they topped an octopus and tomato pasta. They freeze well so keep any leftovers in a small plastic bag, squeeze out the air and freeze for up to 3 months.

for the salad

1 medium potato or 6 new potatoes, skin on

300g squid, cut and scored in pieces to curl up or cut into rings and small tentacles left whole

2 tablespoons extra virgin olive oil

2 spring onions, finely chopped

2 tablespoons salted or brined capers, rinsed well, roughly chopped if large

a large handful of salad leaves

½–1 yellow pepper, cut into thin strips

for the green breadcrumbs

50g white bread from a country-style or gluten-free loaf

20g mixed fresh herbs, such as flat-leaf or curly parsley, marjoram, oregano and thyme leaves

2 tablespoons olive oil

finely grated zest of 1 lemon

for the lemon dressing

4 tablespoons lemon juice

8 tablespoons extra virgin olive oil

salt and freshly ground black pepper

Bring a small pan of salted water to the boil and cook the potato or potatoes until tender. Leave to cool then peel the skin off the medium potato, if using.

Meanwhile, preheat the oven to 150°C/gas mark 2. Line a baking tray with baking parchment.

Whizz the bread and herbs together in a food processor with salt and pepper. Pour into a bowl and mix with the oil and the lemon zest. Transfer the crumbs to the lined tray and roast for about 5 minutes until crisp. Meanwhile, break up the potatoes into bite-sized pieces.

Preheat the grill to high. Mix the squid with the oil, season well and lay onto a grill pan. Cook for 3–5 minutes until just cooked through and lightly browned. Turn halfway through cooking. Toss the remaining salad ingredients with the dressing and arrange on individual plates. Lay over the squid slices and sprinkle over the breadcrumbs to finish.

thai poached prawn, carrot & coriander salad

serves 2–4

This light salad is gorgeous as a starter or as part of a selection of other Vietnamese or Thai salads. It's so quick to make – ready to serve in under 10 minutes. This was shown to us by Susie Jones, who is Cambodian but learned to cook in Thailand. She gave me a holy basil tree (also known as tulsi) and told me to add a few leaves to my salads. It is part of the mint family and is thought to be naturally antibacterial and help reduce stress.

for the salad

175g raw, peeled tiger prawns

½ lemongrass stalk, finely sliced

a few leaves of Thai or Italian basil, finely shredded

leaves from a sprig of holy basil (optional)

1 small carrot, shaved into long lengths

2 radishes, cut into very thin slices

1 garlic clove, finely chopped

1 small red chilli, very finely chopped

2 sprigs of coriander, stems removed, leaves roughly torn

for the dressing

juice of ½ lemon, 1 lime or 1 green lemon

½ teaspoon raw mild honey

¼ teaspoon salt

Cut a slit into the back of each prawn with a sharp knife. Remove the black vein if there is one. This is so that the hot water can penetrate easily into the thicker part of the prawn. Plunge them into a small pan of boiling water for a minute or two until they have just turned pink and then tip into a sieve to drain and cool. Set aside.

Put the dressing ingredients into a large serving bowl, stir well to combine and then add the remaining salad ingredients to the bowl, toss together and serve.

vietnamese spring rolls

serves 6

These light pancake rolls are perfect dunked in the Nuoc Cham Dipping Sauce (page 19) or any dipping sauce. They can be fried in seed or nut oil until golden brown but we prefer them uncooked with the crunchy, raw vegetables inside. For a vegetarian version, add sticks of tofu, beetroot or cucumber, cut into small batons, instead of the prawns. Before making the rolls do a trial one first and taste it to make sure you are happy with the flavour of the herbs, lime and chilli.

50g rice noodles

2 teaspoons flavourless oil, such as grapeseed or groundnut

18 medium spring roll wrappers

a small bunch of coriander, leaves picked and stems discarded

a small bunch of mint, leaves picked and stems discarded

1 medium carrot, coarsely grated

225g cooked, peeled king prawns

juice of 1 lime

3 tablespoons chilli sauce or 2 teaspoons finely chopped red
    or green chilli

Nuoc Cham Dipping Sauce (page 19), to serve

Soak the noodles in plenty of boiling water for 8–10 minutes or until soft. Drain and rinse well in cold water. Toss with the oil to stop them sticking together and set aside.

Put a wet cloth, such as a flannel or tea towel, onto a large plate and assemble all the ingredients in piles in front of you on a clean work surface. Press one wrapper down onto the cloth to moisten and soften it. Make a rectangular pile of a little coriander, mint, carrot and some prawns on the wrapper just below centre, squeeze over a little lime juice and splash over a little chilli sauce. Roll the wrapper halfway, tuck the ends in and continue to roll up to secure the filling inside. Repeat to fill the remaining wrappers. Serve with Nuoc Cham Dipping Sauce.

beetroot & salmon tiradito

serves 6

Tiradito is similar to ceviche, although it wasn't always that way. Originally the fish in ceviche was cubed and in tiradito it was sliced, now, since the immigration of thousands of Japanese in the 19th century, ceviche is also commonly sliced. Tiradito is lighter than ceviche and the tiger's milk doesn't usually contain onion. The sauce is served at the table so each diner pours it over the fish just before eating.

This recipe is from the marvellous young chef Adam Rawson. Although he uses imported ingredients such as plantain and giant corn he also likes to mix in European produce, such as horseradish instead of wasabi, and beetroots as they add crunch and have a natural sweetness to balance the sour lime juice.

for the tiradito

½ small red onion, finely chopped

1 medium beetroot, cut into 1cm dice

½–1 red chilli, according to taste, finely sliced

juice of 1 lime

400g very fresh salmon fillet, pin-boned, skinned and thinly sliced

1 avocado

sea salt flakes

2 tablespoons extra virgin olive oil

a small handful of leaves, such as baby beetroot, watercress
   or sprouted cress

1 teaspoon black onion seeds

salt and freshly ground black pepper

for the beetroot tiger's milk

250ml beetroot juice

juice of 2 limes

2 tablespoons soy sauce

1 tablespoon rice vinegar

1–2 teaspoons wasabi powder or sauce or
   1–2 teaspoons finely grated horseradish, according to taste

finely grated horseradish, to garnish (optional)

Soak the chopped onion in cold water.

Pour the beetroot juice into a large frying pan over a low heat and reduce by one-third to about 160ml, pour into a jug and set aside to cool.

Toss the beetroot cubes with the chilli, half the lime juice, salt and pepper.

Add the remaining tiger's milk ingredients to the beetroot juice in the jug. Season to taste with salt and pepper and wasabi (or horseradish) until you have a tangy, hot sauce. This can be done a day in advance.

Lay the salmon onto individual plates or shallow bowls. Thinly slice the avocado and lay onto the plates, squeeze over the remaining lime juice to stop the slices from browning. Put the plates into the fridge or a cool place until you are ready to serve.

Just before serving, season the fish and avocado with salt and freshly ground black pepper and drizzle over the olive oil. Arrange a little pile of beetroot cubes topped with the leaves on the plates and scatter over the onion seeds and onions. Serve straight away, with the tiger's milk on the side and garnished with horseradish, if you like.

simple sea bream, grape & celery ceviche

serves 6 as a starter

Another of Adam Rawson's recipes from his travels in Lima, this simple ceviche is a mixture of lime juice, chilli and salt which 'cooks' thinly cut fish in minutes, turning it from translucent pinkish grey to opaque white. The proteins are denatured with the acid of the citrus fruit, giving the fish a cooked texture.

It is really important the fish is fresh, so ask your fishmonger for the latest delivery. Many restaurants freeze the fish for 24 hours at -20°C before using it to kill any possible parasites. This is difficult in a domestic freezer but a fishmonger can do this for you and a lot of fish sold in supermarkets is previously frozen.

Whole corn on the cob is often served on the side or a bowl of toasted fat kernels, which gives a welcome sweetness after the punchy citrus and salt in the ceviche.

4 x approx. 125g fillets very fresh sea bream, sea bass or haddock, pin-boned and skinned

½–1 teaspoon celery salt

juice of 2 limes

2 celery sticks, finely sliced on the diagonal, plus a small handful of celery leaves

100g green seedless grapes, halved

¼–½ jalapeño chilli or hot green chilli, according to taste, finely sliced

a small handful of coriander leaves, roughly chopped

1 teaspoon pink peppercorns, lightly crushed

Slice the fish at a 45° angle with a sharp knife across the fillet so that you end up with pieces about 3mm thick. Lay the slices onto a serving plate.

Scatter over the celery salt and pour over the lime juice. Top with the chopped celery and leaves, grapes, chilli, coriander leaves and lightly crushed pink peppercorns and serve straight away.

sea bass, lime & coriander ceviche

serves 6 as a starter

This recipe is from Adam Rawson, former head chef of Pachamama, a modern Peruvian restaurant. Peruvians like to eat ceviche in the mornings, keeping the food light and fresh. A shot of tiger's milk, the leftover marinating liquid, can be drunk on its own; apparently it's a local hangover cure! Tiger's milk has evolved from a simple combination of lime and salt to recipes including ground fish bones, citrus fruits, sometimes garlic and other aromatics. It should be plentiful on the plate or in the bowl; it needs to coat the fish to work its magic, so be generous.

When making ceviche, remember to balance the flavours; as well as the acidity of the citrus there is usually something sweet, such as kernels of corn, beetroot or cubes of steamed sweet potato.

for the ceviche

½ small red onion, finely chopped (use the other half for the tiger's milk)

1 small sweet potato, cut into 1cm dice

sea salt flakes and freshly ground black pepper

2 tablespoons extra virgin olive oil

4 x approx. 125g fillets very fresh sea bass or sea bream, pin-boned and skinned

4 baby radishes, shaved

½–1 red chilli, according to taste, finely sliced (use any leftover for the tiger's milk)

a small handful of raw samphire or rocket

salt and freshly ground black pepper

coriander leaves, to garnish

for the tiger's milk

juice of 2 limes

½ small red onion

¼–½ red chilli, according to taste

1 lemongrass stalk

1 tomato

1 celery stick

2cm piece of fresh root ginger, peeled

1 small garlic clove

½ teaspoon salt

Preheat the oven to 200°C/gas mark 6. Soak the finely chopped onion in cold water.

Whizz the tiger's milk ingredients together in a blender until smooth. Leave to stand for 15 minutes and then strain into a lidded jar. Keep in the fridge until needed. This can be done up to a day in advance.

Season the sweet potato with salt and freshly ground black pepper and toss in the olive oil. Transfer to a baking tray and cook for 15 minutes or until just tender and lightly golden. Set aside to cool.

Slice the fish at a 45° angle with a sharp knife across the fillet so that you end up with pieces about 3mm thick – this is the method used to slice smoked salmon by hand. Lay the slices onto a plate in a single layer. Set aside in the fridge.

Drain the onion and toss onto kitchen paper to dry. Tip into a large bowl with the sweet potato, radishes, chilli and samphire. Toss together gently to combine.

Remove the fish from the fridge and scatter over a little salt and pepper. Leave for 15 seconds, then pour over the tiger's milk – making sure that all the pieces of fish are coated in it (any leftover milk will keep for a couple of days in the fridge). The fish will turn opaque in about 5 minutes. Top with the salad, garnish with the coriander leaves and serve straight away.

the dip of joy

serves 10–12

A fun name for a seriously good starter given to this über dip by some girlfriends. One of them, Karin, showed me how to make it for a party. Layers of soft guacamole and soured cream lie on top of creamy refried beans, topped with spicy tomato salsa, grated cheese and salad ready to be dipped into with crunchy homemade tortilla chips. To save time you can buy the refried beans but do make your own guacamole and salsa, it's worth it.

for the refried beans

3 tablespoons extra virgin olive oil

1 large onion, finely chopped

3 garlic cloves, roughly chopped

leaves from 2 sprigs of thyme

2 x 400g cans black or pinto beans, drained or 480g cooked
   weight from dried black or pinto beans, drained

salt and freshly ground black pepper

for the dips & chips

16–20 soft large tortillas

100ml extra virgin olive oil

1 quantity of Guacamole (page 182)

300ml carton soured cream

1 quantity of Spicy Tomato Salsa (page 171)

150g mature Cheddar or Red Leicester cheese, coarsely grated

a handful of coriander leaves, roughly chopped

For the refried beans, heat the oil in a heavy-based pan and when hot fry the onion over a low heat with seasoning until soft. This should take about 10 minutes. Halfway through the cooking time add the garlic and thyme and cook until soft. Add the cooked beans and the 200ml water (use the cooking water if you cooked them from dried) and bring to the boil. Use a potato masher or stick blender to crush the beans to a chunky purée, adding a little more water if needed until you have a thick dip. Taste and season again as necessary. Remove from the heat and leave to cool to room temperature.

To cook the tortillas, preheat the oven to 200°C/gas mark 6. Cut the tortillas into strips about 5cm wide, some will be long and some short. Spread them out onto baking trays. Brush with the olive oil and season with salt and pepper. Cook until firm and crisp but not brittle or they will break. It should take about 5 minutes for them to become golden brown.

To assemble the dip of joy, either make up individual dishes or one big glass bowl – I use a large, wide fruit bowl. First spread the refried beans over the bottom of the dish and follow this with the guacamole and then the soured cream. Next add the salsa followed by the grated cheese. Top it all with coriander and serve, within the hour, with the tortilla chips.

tip

To cook black or pinto beans from dried, allow 240g dried beans to obtain cooked weight of approx. 480g. Soak them overnight in plenty of cold water. Bring the beans to the boil in fresh water and cook until tender. Drain, but reserve the cooking water.

shaved manchego, celeriac & radish salad with white truffle oil

serves 4–6

This is a salad for all seasons, as any vegetable that can be cut into light, almost transparent ribbons is suitable for this assembly of flavours and textures. The Manchego (or Pecorino, as it is still a sheep's cheese) seems to enhance the flavours of the vegetables, helping them stand up to the precious drops of truffle-scented oil and the crumbled walnuts. Try Jerusalem artichoke and pear, various types of mushroom or carrot and beetroot and experiment with other oils such as walnut, or avocado, or simply enjoy a good single estate olive oil.

50g walnut halves

12 asparagus spears

⅓ small celeriac

6 radishes

75g Manchego cheese

3 tablespoons extra virgin olive oil

a few drops of white truffle oil

salt and freshly ground black pepper

Preheat the oven to 180°C/gas mark 4 and toast the walnuts on a baking tray for 6 minutes or until just browned.

Cut the vegetables and cheese into thin ribbons and slices using a potato peeler, mandoline or very sharp knife. Pile a single layer onto a serving platter and season with salt and pepper, splash over a little olive oil and a few drops of truffle oil. Repeat the layers until all the ingredients are used up.

To finish, lightly crush the walnuts using a pestle and mortar or roughly chop with a knife and scatter over the salad. Finish with a twist of black pepper and serve.

endive, piquillo pepper & chorizo salad

serves 4

Crunchy endive leaves are the perfect foil for smoky chorizo and sweet peppers. These Catalan flavours come from our good friend and teacher Carolina Català-Fortuny. She makes this on her tapas course and serves it in a bowl with more whole endive leaves for scooping up the salad.

2 x approx. 85g cooking chorizo, sliced or crumbled

6 piquillo peppers from a jar, drained and cut into thin strips

2 garlic cloves, finely chopped

12 Kalamata-style black olives, pitted and halved

1 tablespoon chopped flat-leaf parsley

2 tablespoons dry sherry

3 white endives

1 tablespoon sherry vinegar

3 tablespoons extra virgin olive oil

salt and freshly ground black pepper

Cook the chorizo in a cold frying pan over a medium heat until the fat has rendered and it starts browning slightly. Add the peppers, garlic, olives and parsley and cook together for a few minutes. Add the dry sherry and cook until it has reduced, about 3–4 minutes. Remove from the heat and set aside.

Remove 8–10 of the outer layers of the endives and set aside. Chop the rest of the endives into 1cm strips, discarding the woody ends, and mix with the cooked chorizo and peppers.

Make the dressing by mixing the vinegar and oil together, season with salt and pepper to taste; remember the chorizo is quite salty.

To finish off the dish, arrange the whole endive leaves all around a serving platter and place the pepper, chorizo and endive mixture in the centre. Drizzle with the dressing and serve.

3

salads from the farm

old english sallet of torn chicken with oranges & barberries

tabbouleh with pulled lamb shoulder with a spiced date crust & minted labneh

peach & lentil salad with warm pork tenderloin

coronation chicken with lychees

warm smoked ham hock & celery salad with marmalade & ginger dressing

pineapple & cashew rice salad with hula pork & roast peppers

windfall slaw with crispy southern chicken & chipotle cream

chicken shawarma, lettuce & coriander salad with lemon crème fraîche

guinea fowl & artichoke salad with harissa sauce

shredded chicken & cabbage salad

fruity salad & korean roasted duck with five-spice marinade

confit duck, crispy potato & garlic salad

asian rainbow slaw with korean beef in lettuce wraps

mexican beef salad

rare steak tagliata, salsa verde, charred onions, tomato salad

greek lemon chicken, grain & feta salad with tzatziki

old english sallet of torn chicken with oranges & barberries

serves 6

While perusing old salad recipes I came across *Acetaria: A Discourse of Sallets* by John Evelyn. Published in 1699, he talks of wonderful 'sallets' made from a huge variety of herbs, flowers, berries and fruits as well as oil and vinegar dressings. Far more inspired than your average mixed salad today.

One of Evelyn's simpler salads is perfect for softly poached chicken leftover from making stock or from a roast. Barberries and green sultanas are available online, in good delis or Middle Eastern shops. They were once used regularly in salads and have a pleasant sourness that adds bite and texture. If you can't find barberries, use unsweetened dried cranberries instead.

for the dressing

2 tablespoons red wine or cider vinegar

5 tablespoons extra virgin olive oil or mild rapeseed oil

1 tablespoon wholegrain mustard

1–2 teaspoons raw mild honey, to taste

salt and freshly ground black pepper

for the salad

500g cooked chicken, shredded

3 tablespoons dried barberries, soaked in cold water for 30 minutes

3 tablespoons tarragon leaves

2 tablespoons roughly torn flat-leaf parsley leaves

a large handful of salad leaves, such as purslane, salad burnet
   or watercress

25g flaked almonds, toasted

25g golden or green sultanas, soaked in cold water for 30 minutes

2 oranges, segmented

Mix the dressing ingredients together and adjust the seasoning to taste.

Combine the salad ingredients in a large serving bowl and pour over the dressing. Toss to mingle the flavours together and leave to stand for 30 minutes. Dress with a little black pepper before serving.

tabbouleh with pulled lamb shoulder with a spiced date crust & minted labneh

serves 6–8

This is inspired by the Moroccan way of cooking meat with dried fruits. Often a clarified butter called smen is used, but for ease we've used plain salted butter. The dates, butter and spices form a sticky, sweet and spicy crust on the lamb which is gorgeous with a yogurt and mint sauce on salad leaves. Serve with Quinoa Kabsa with Nut Hashu (page 164), Fattoush (page 161), Moroccan Crushed Aubergine & Tomato (page 159) and Ginger Vichy Carrot Salad (page 181). If you don't have hot paprika, add 1 teaspoon of dried chilli flakes. Don't be tempted to use smoked paprika as it overwhelms the lamb.

This is our friend Amal's tabbouleh. Her family scoop it up with lettuce leaves which are traditionally tucked into the edge of the dish before serving. I was surprised to see how little bulgar wheat she added; it is really more of a parsley salad. For a gluten-free version use quinoa instead. Tabbouleh varies according to the seasons – this is a summer version. In winter remove the tomatoes and spring onions and add grated celeriac, slices of fennel, crushed walnuts and pomegranate seeds.

for the lamb

1 medium to large bone-in shoulder of lamb, weighing about 2kg

10 Medjool dates, pitted

100g butter

5 garlic cloves, crushed

2 teaspoons fresh or dried thyme leaves

2 teaspoons dried oregano

2 teaspoons ground cinnamon

2 teaspoons hot paprika

½–1 teaspoon chilli powder, according to taste

1½ teaspoons salt, plus extra

freshly ground black pepper

for the tabbouleh

100g coarse bulgar wheat or quinoa (for a gluten-free option)

a very large handful (about 35g) of flat-leaf parsley, finely chopped

200g ripe cherry or round tomatoes, roughly chopped, plus a few
    to garnish

125g cucumber, peeled and cubed

5 spring onions, ½ red onion or ½ shallot

a small handful of mint, finely chopped, plus 10 leaves, roughly torn,
    to garnish

2 Little Gem lettuces, trimmed and split into leaves

for the dressing

1 garlic clove, finely chopped

juice of 1 lemon

4 tablespoons olive oil

3 tablespoons pomegranate molasses

1 tablespoon red wine vinegar

1 teaspoon sumac

1 teaspoon sugar (optional)

for the minted labneh

300ml yogurt or Labneh (page 202)

a small handful of mint, finely chopped

a small handful of flat-leaf parsley, finely chopped

1 garlic clove, finely chopped

a few pieces of red chilli, finely chopped

a handful of roughly chopped walnuts and/or pine nuts and chilli
    powder, to garnish

 If using quinoa.

Preheat the oven to 220°C/gas mark 7. Allow the lamb to come to room temperature; this should take about 30 minutes and will ensure the lamb cooks evenly. Cut away any tough leathery skin from the top; white waxy fat is good so leave that.

Prepare the date crust by blending the dates, butter, garlic, herbs, spices, 1 teaspoon of salt and freshly ground black pepper with 200ml water using a stick blender, food processor, or chop by hand. It will be thick and sticky. Season the lamb shoulder on the raggedy underside and lay onto an oven tray. Make sure the top surface is dry or pat with kitchen paper. Coat the top and sides with the date crust by spreading it out with a palette knife or the back of a spoon. Use all of the crust mixture.

Pour 200ml cold water into the tray. Wrap it tightly in 2 layers of foil and bake for 10 minutes. Reduce the temperature to 170°C/gas mark 3 and roast for 2 hours. Remove the lamb from the oven and remove a corner of the foil (carefully, as the steam rushes out) and check to see if it is dry. If there are no juices under the lamb add another 100ml water and wrap up again. Cook for a further hour. To test if the meat is done, pull the shoulder bone away slightly. The meat around it should give easily, be tender and about to fall off the bone. If it is not done to your liking replace the foil and return the lamb to the oven (this can happen if the shoulder is very large).

To make the tabbouleh, soak the bulgar wheat in boiling water for 10 minutes or until soft. Drain and leave to cool spread on a plate. If using quinoa, cook according to packet instructions and cool as above.

Combine the dressing ingredients in a jug, mix well and season to taste. If it's too citrusy add a teaspoon of sugar and mix well.

Put the bulgar wheat or quinoa into a large bowl and add the remaining ingredients, except the lettuce leaves. Pour over the dressing and gently combine. Put onto a serving platter with the extra mint and cherry tomatoes on top. Arrange lettuce leaves around the outside to scoop up the tabbouleh.

To make the minted labneh, mix the ingredients together in a bowl and season to taste. Put in a bowl and garnish with nuts and chilli powder then transfer to the fridge to chill.

Remove the lamb from the roasting pan and set aside on a plate to rest, covered in foil and a couple of cloths to keep it warm. Leave it to rest for at least 20 minutes – it can be left up to 45 minutes before serving. Then take two forks and pull the meat from the bone and transfer to a warmed serving dish. The sweet bark-like coating will flake into bits with the lean meat. Serve the lamb with the minted labneh and tabbouleh.

peach & lentil salad with warm pork tenderloin

serves 4–6

Pork and fennel seeds have been a classic combination in Italy since ancient Roman times. Wild fennel grows abundantly and produces masses of yellow flowers that are gathered for fennel pollen or left to mature until the seeds form. It always amazes me that Italians grow it to eat and in the UK we grow it mainly for beauty. We believe you can do both. Wild fennel is often to be seen in the UK but many people don't realise it can be eaten and instead enjoy looking at the feathery fronds. Ahh, the difference between the Italians and the English!

1 tablespoon fennel seeds
1 garlic clove, finely chopped
1 teaspoon fine sea salt
1 x 600g pork tenderloin
1 tablespoon extra virgin olive oil

for the dressing
juice of 1 lemon
4 tablespoons extra virgin olive oil
salt and freshly ground black pepper

for the salad
390g can Puy or bijoux verts lentils, rinsed and drained
60g soft dried prunes, roughly chopped
2 tablespoons finely chopped flat-leaf parsley
75g spinach, kale, lettuce, mustard leaves or rocket
2 peaches, stoned, skin on and each one cut into 12 slices
2 tablespoons chopped dill or wild fennel

Crush the fennel seeds using a pestle and mortar and sprinkle them over a piece of baking parchment with the garlic and salt. Trim any tough silverskin from the tenderloin and roll it in the garlic, salt and crushed fennel seeds on the paper. Roll up in the parchment, place on a plate and transfer to the fridge for at least 30 minutes and up to a day.

Preheat the oven to 180°C/gas mark 4. Remove the pork from the fridge to come to room temperature while you make the salad.

For the dressing, combine the lemon juice and oil in a bowl and season to taste.

For the salad, the lentils should be at room temperature or lightly warmed in a pan over a low heat. Mix the lentils, prunes and parsley together, add half the dressing and toss to combine – keep the remaining dressing for the last minute before serving. Arrange the lentils on a large platter with the leaves, peach slices and dill.

Heat the oil in a large non-stick frying pan and when hot brown the pork all over to seal in the juices. Transfer to a roasting tin and cook for 12–15 minutes or until it is firm to the touch. Remove from the oven and set aside, covered in foil and a tea-towel, to rest for 10 minutes. Cut into approx. 1cm slices, arrange on top of the lentils with any cooking juices and the reserved dressing poured over the top. Serve straight away.

coronation chicken with lychees

serves 6–8

Coronation chicken was possibly the first TV dinner. It was originally created by Rosemary Hume in the 1950s for people to eat while glued to their black and white televisions to watch the coronation of Queen Elizabeth II.

The ingredients are easy to find and it's always delicious. It can be made with leftover cooked turkey or chicken, in which case simply miss out cooking the meat at the beginning. We often use the meat left over from boiling a whole chicken or couple of turkey legs in water when making stock. Then we spice the stock and use this for cooking couscous or rice for the Quinoa Kabsa (page 164). Bright orange dried apricots have been exposed to sulphur-dioxide gas to preserve their colour so we prefer to use organic dried apricots that are darker in colour.

Coronation chicken is traditionally served with lettuce leaves around the edge but it is also lovely with one of the Indian dishes on pages 144–145.

for the chicken

1 carrot, sliced in half lengthways

2 celery hearts, with leaves or just a handful of celery leaves

1 small white onion, halved

1 bay leaf

900g boneless, skinless chicken breasts or thighs or 900g cooked chicken

for the salad

25g flaked almonds

150g organic dried apricots, cut into thirds

400g can lychees, drained and torn into quarters

a small handful of fresh coriander, roughly chopped, thick stalks discarded

for the dressing

500g live natural thick yogurt

300ml mayonnaise, homemade (page 21) or shop-bought

3 tablespoons medium curry powder

salt and freshly ground black pepper

Put the carrot, celery, onion and bay leaf in a large saucepan and add enough cold water to cover them by 10cm. Put a lid on and bring to the boil, then add the uncooked chicken. Return to the boil and cook, uncovered, until tender. This will take about 15 minutes for chicken breast meat or 20–25 minutes for thighs, depending on their size. It is best to keep them whole while cooking so as not to lose flavour. When done, drain and set aside to cool. Tear the meat into bite-sized pieces.

Toast the almonds in a dry pan or in an oven at 180°C/gas mark 4 for about 5 minutes or until they start to become golden brown. Toss a couple of times during the cooking.

Mix the dressing ingredients together and season to taste.

Add the chicken to the dressing with the apricots, lychees and coriander and scatter the almonds on top.

warm smoked ham hock & celery salad with marmalade & ginger dressing

serves 6

This is an ideal salad for a cold winter day inspired by Sarah Randell's marmalade dressing from her delightful book *Marmalade: A Bittersweet Cookbook*. We have added grated ginger to it for a little warmth and background spice.

Pot barley is our grain of choice for this salad – we like its nutty, chewy quality – but it can easily be substituted by another that you have in the cupboard. Pot barley is best soaked overnight, so be prepared. Serve as it is or with a wedge of Seville orange to squeeze over. We also like this with pickled walnuts.

150g pot or pearl barley, farro or quinoa (for a gluten-free option)
1.5 litres ham stock or 1.5 litres water mixed with 1 teaspoon salt
300g cooked smoked ham
4 spring onions, finely chopped
2 celery sticks and leaves, finely sliced on the diagonal
a handful of flat-leaf parsley, roughly chopped

for the dressing
zest and juice of 1 lemon or 1 Seville orange, plus extra to taste
juice of 1 sweet orange
3 tablespoons olive oil
3 tablespoons Seville orange or lemon marmalade
4 teaspoons grated fresh root ginger, plus extra to taste
salt and freshly ground black pepper

  If using quinoa.

Soak the barley overnight in enough cold water to cover by 5cm.

Drain the barley and put into a large saucepan. Add the ham stock or salted water – it should cover the barley by 5cm – and cook for 15–20 minutes until tender. If using any of the other grains, cook using the stock or salted water, following the packet instructions. Drain the grains and leave to cool to room temperature.

Tear the cooked ham into bite-sized shreds, discarding any skin or fat. Put this into a large mixing bowl with the remaining salad ingredients and the grains when at room temperature.

To make the dressing, mix all the ingredients together in a bowl, chopping any really big pieces of orange rind with a pair of scissors. You want little bursts of orange marmalade flavour through the salad. Season to taste, adding more ginger, lemon or orange juice to achieve a punchy flavour that is not too sweet.

Mix the dressing with the salad and season again as necessary. Serve straight away at room temperature. Alternatively, transfer the salad to the fridge until ready to serve – this will give the barley a chance to soak up the wonderful flavours. To serve, warm the salad briefly in a microwave for 5 minutes or covered in foil in a preheated oven at 180°C/gas mark 4 for 20 minutes.

pineapple & cashew rice salad with hula pork & roast peppers

serves 6

for the pork

500ml pineapple juice

2 teaspoons finely grated fresh ginger

2 fat garlic cloves, finely grated

150ml soy sauce or tamari

150ml tomato ketchup

4 tablespoons cider vinegar

1–2 tablespoons Sriracha sauce or other hot sauce, according to taste

2–2.5kg boned pork shoulder

3 red peppers, cut into 8 long strips

2 tablespoons extra virgin olive oil

salt and freshly ground black pepper

for the pineapple & cashew rice salad

300g wholegrain rice

4 cardamom pods, split open

1 teaspoon salt

25g shredded or shaved coconut

100g cashews, soaked in cold water for minimum 30 minutes and overnight if possible

300g fresh pineapple, cut into 5mm thick slices

2 tablespoons coconut or extra virgin olive oil

8 spring onions, sliced on the diagonal into 2cm lengths

a handful of coriander leaves, roughly chopped, to serve

a handful of flat-leaf parsley leaves, roughly chopped, to serve

This is a family favourite; pork shoulder bathed in a warm bath of sticky sweet pineapple sauce. It is cooked until it falls apart then pulled and served with a rice salad. This version is based on one by Tieghan Gerard, a passionate young blogger from www.halfbakedharvest.com who serves her hula pork on tacos.

The colourful salad is a great fruity, crunchy partner to the pulled meat and requires only a splash of olive oil. It is good enough to eat on its own as a vegetarian or vegan option. Drizzle with the Sesame Ginger Soy Dressing (page 18).

Preheat the oven to 180°C/gas mark 4.

Mix the pineapple juice, ginger, garlic, soy sauce, tomato ketchup, vinegar and Sriracha together and season to taste. If the shoulder is tied into a roll, untie it. Put it into a large casserole dish and pour over the sauce, making sure it goes into every crevice of the pork. Put on the lid and cook for 3–4 hours, depending on the weight of the pork, or until it is very tender. About 30 minutes before the end of cooking time, pop the peppers onto a tray and splash with the oil and seasoning. Cook until lightly browned.

Remove the pork from the oven and transfer it to a board. Pour the sauce into a serving jug. Use two forks to 'pull' the meat, tearing it into shreds. This can be done the day before. To reheat the meat and peppers, put them into a shallow ovenproof dish with a little of the sauce and cover with foil. Reheat in a preheated oven at 180°C/gas mark 4 for 20–30 minutes or until piping hot.

Cook the rice, with the cardamom and salt, following the packet instructions. Drain and set aside to cool.

Meanwhile, toast the coconut and cashews separately on a baking tray in the oven (the coconut is quicker to cook) until lightly browned. Keep an eye on them as they burn easily and will be done in 5 minutes or so. This can also be done in a dry frying pan.

Toast the pineapple under a preheated grill or in a dry griddle pan until golden and lightly charred, about 7–10 minutes, then set aside to cool. Cut into bite-sized pieces, discarding the centre core. Heat the oil in a small frying pan and cook the spring onions for 5–7 minutes until softened and set aside to cool. As soon as all the remaining ingredients for the rice are at room temperature, mix them together with the herbs. Season to taste.

Serve the rice salad straight away with the pulled pork and roasted peppers and with the remaining sauce in a jug.

Alternatively, cover the salad and chill in the fridge for up to a day. Let the salad come to room temperature before serving alongside the pork and peppers.

windfall slaw with crispy southern chicken & chipotle cream

serves 6

Giancarlo's guilty pleasure has long been fried chicken. As he is now gluten-free we were determined to find a way to satiate his need for the finger-licking fried stuff. This recipe is based on one by Barry C. Parsons at www.rockrecipes.com.

We use a mixture of dried and fresh herbs as we hate to use dried when we have fresh in the garden. If you don't have one, simply leave it out. This fruity Windfall Slaw is a good way to use up apples and pears that have dropped from the trees. The Charred Corn & Avocado Salad (page 167) also goes well here.

First mix together the buttermilk, mustard, salt, pepper and paprika in a bowl. Pour it into a large plastic food bag (or a container with a lid) with the chicken and seal well. Leave the bag in the fridge for a minimum of 2 hours and preferably overnight. Turn the bag a couple of times to ensure the chicken is evenly coated.

Toast the peanuts in a dry pan over a medium heat until lightly browned. Set aside to cool and then roughly chop. Combine all the slaw ingredients in a large mixing bowl. Season to taste, adding a little extra pickling vinegar if you like a little punch.

Make the chipotle cream by mixing the ingredients together and adjust the heat with more chipotle or cream as necessary.

Preheat the oven to 180°C/gas mark 4. Line a baking sheet with a silicone mat or baking parchment.

Gather the fresh herbs, if using, and garlic together on a chopping board and finely chop them with a sharp knife. Put them into a bowl with the remaining coating ingredients. Remove the chicken from the bag and dip all the pieces into the coating mixture, making sure they are well covered. Put them on the lined baking sheet.

Now spray the chicken pieces with oil spray, as suggested by Barry, or drizzle over the oil, and bake for about 20 minutes for the breast meat pieces and 30–40 minutes for the bone-in pieces. To be sure the chicken is cooked through, test the internal temperature with a meat thermometer – it should be 74°C. If you don't have one, pierce the thickest part of the chicken with a skewer and make sure the juices that run out are clear. Serve the chicken with the slaw, chipotle cream and gherkins on the side.

for the chicken
250ml buttermilk
1 tablespoon Dijon mustard
1 teaspoon salt
1 teaspoon freshly ground black pepper
1 teaspoon paprika
1.5kg bone-in chicken pieces or breast meat
olive oil spray or 4 tablespoons olive oil

for the windfall slaw
50g unsalted peanuts
200g red cabbage, finely shredded
1 apple, skin on and cut into sticks
1 pear, skin on and cut into sticks
2 celery sticks, finely sliced
2 tablespoons pickled jalapeño slices, drained
a small handful of fresh coriander, stems discarded
1 small red onion, finely sliced
2 tablespoons juice from the jalapeños or lemon juice or vinegar
4 tablespoons extra virgin olive oil
juice of 1 lime
salt and freshly ground black pepper

for the chipotle cream
1 teaspoon chipotle paste
100ml soured cream
50ml mayonnaise, homemade (page 21) or shop-bought

for the coating
1 teaspoon dried or fresh thyme leaves, stripped from the stems
2 tablespoons dried or fresh roughly chopped sage leaves, stripped from the stems
2 garlic cloves
100g plain or gluten-free flour
3 tablespoons dried oregano
1 tablespoon mustard powder
1 tablespoon ground ginger
1 tablespoon hot (unsmoked) paprika
2 teaspoons salt
1 teaspoon freshly ground black pepper
½–1 teaspoon chilli powder, according to taste

sliced gherkins, to serve

chicken shawarma, lettuce & coriander salad with lemon crème fraîche

serves 6

'Shawarma' means 'turning' in Turkish and this is best made from fatty cuts of meat like thighs, which are constantly turned over a heat source, so the skin and fat constantly baste the lean meat. We love this chicken the way my sister Louise showed me; she serves it cut into strips and stuffed into warm pitta breads with lemon crème fraîche, a simple shredded lettuce salad and green olives. Alternatively, do as they do in Turkish kebab shops and offer a selection of accompaniments for people to make their own, such as flat-leaf parsley and mint leaves, chilli sauce, pickled green chillies, the Aioli (page 21) or Tahini Citrus Dressing (page 18).

for the marinade

juice of 2 lemons

75ml olive oil

5 garlic cloves, grated

2 teaspoons ground cumin

3 teaspoons sweet paprika

1 teaspoon ground coriander

1 teaspoon salt

½ teaspoon freshly ground black pepper

1 teaspoon ground cinnamon

¼–½ teaspoon dried chilli flakes, according to taste

½ teaspoon ground turmeric

for the chicken

1kg boneless, skin-on chicken thighs

2 red onions, each cut into 8 wedges

for the lemon crème fraîche

200ml crème fraîche

finely grated zest of ½–1 lemon, according to taste

1–2 teaspoons lemon juice, according to taste

for the salad

300g romaine lettuce, very finely shredded

3 spring onions or a small shallot, thinly sliced

2 tablespoons coriander, tough stalks discarded and the rest roughly torn

¼–½ finely chopped red or green chilli, according to taste (optional)

juice of 1 lemon

3 tablespoons extra virgin olive oil

pitta bread (optional) and green olives, to serve

salt and freshly ground black pepper

 If not using the pitta bread.

Mix together all the marinade ingredients in a large bowl. Add the chicken and onions and toss in the marinade. Cover and leave in the fridge for at least 1 hour and overnight if possible.

Meanwhile, make the lemon crème fraîche by mixing the ingredients together, taste and adjust the seasoning as necessary. Decant into a bowl and set aside in the fridge.

When you are ready to cook, preheat the oven to 220°C/gas mark 7. Line a baking tray with a silicone mat or baking parchment.

Lay the chicken pieces onto the prepared tray, spacing them out, then pour over any leftover sauce. Roast for 30–40 minutes or until the chicken is cooked through. To be sure the chicken is cooked through, test the internal temperature with a meat thermometer – it should be 74°C. If you don't have a meat thermometer, pierce the thickest part of the chicken with a skewer and check that the juices are clear and not pink. Remove the chicken from the oven and use a knife and fork to cut it into shreds. If the skin is crispy we like to shred it and mix it with the chicken.

Prepare the salad by tossing the ingredients together in a bowl. Season to taste.

Carefully pour away the oil from the tray and pour the cooking juices into a warm jug. Arrange the pieces on a wooden board, with the jug, salad, lemon crème fraîche, olives and pitta bread.

guinea fowl & artichoke salad with harissa sauce

serves 4–6

I prefer the stronger flavour of guinea fowl to chicken and try to use it whenever I see it for this Moorish inspired salad. For a vegetarian version use feta instead or a little crumbled over the top with the meat is lovely. If you can find small tender artichokes, prepare and cook these, but we often use the ready-cooked canned variety in brine. If you can only find artichokes in oil, rinse them thoroughly to get rid of the marinade. We serve this warm in winter and at room temperature in summer. It is also good the next day. The harissa is delicious so I often make double and keep some for roast meats or vegetables.

400g can artichoke hearts, drained, or 160g artichokes in oil, drained weight

1 guinea fowl, jointed into 8 pieces or 6 boneless, skin-on chicken thighs

1 aubergine, cut into 2cm cubes

1 red pepper, deseeded and cut into 8 long strips

50g sun-dried tomatoes in oil, drained weight, cut into 1cm slices

1 red onion, cut into 8 wedges

100ml extra virgin olive oil

200g white or brown rice, barley, quinoa or freekeh

½ teaspoon saffron strands

30g flat-leaf parsley, stems discarded, roughly chopped

juice of ½ lemon

salt and freshly ground black pepper

for the harissa sauce

1 teaspoon cumin seeds

1 teaspoon caraway seeds

1 teaspoon coriander seeds

1 tablespoon tomato purée

2 tablespoons extra virgin olive oil

½–1 teaspoon dried chilli flakes, according to taste

2 tablespoons lemon juice

a large handful of soft salad leaves, such as lamb's lettuce or spinach and lemon wedges, to serve

Preheat the oven to 200°C/gas mark 6. Wash the artichokes well in cold water, especially if they have been in strong-tasting oil, and set aside to drain. If not already cut, slice each artichoke in half.

Season the guinea fowl or chicken pieces all over with salt and pepper and put in a roasting dish. Put the artichoke halves, aubergine, pepper, tomatoes and onion around the meat and pour over 75ml of the oil. Roast for 30–40 minutes or until the meat is cooked through. Remove from the oven and leave to cool to warm rather than hot.

To make the harissa sauce, toast the seeds in a dry frying pan until they start to pop and become fragrant. Remove from the heat and grind using a pestle and mortar or a spice grinder until you have a fine powder. Tip into a bowl and mix with the remaining sauce ingredients, season and adjust the flavour, to taste, with chilli and lemon juice. Set aside. This will keep in the fridge for up to a week if topped with a little olive oil to form a seal.

Cook the rice, or your chosen grain, with the saffron strands, according to the packet instructions. Toss the rice or grain with the parsley, lemon juice and remaining oil and spoon onto a large platter or wooden board.

Lay the cooked meat and vegetables on top of the rice and pour the juices from the baking tray over the top. Add the leaves to the platter with the lemon wedges and serve with the harissa sauce on the side.

shredded chicken & cabbage salad

serves 6

This salad (photographed on page 104) is from Susie Jones, a Cambodian chef who loves using local produce in her South East Asian cooking. Instead of jicama (a firm root vegetable with a mild fruity flavour) or green mango you can use raw swede, a firm slightly sour plum or a yellow pepper. As long as everything is raw and good to eat, most vegetables or firm unripe fruits will work with this dressing. It is the same for the herbs – add what you have available. If you are out of coriander just add more mint.

For a twist use the juice from 4 kumquats in the dressing instead of the lemon juice to give a mild orange flavour. Try to find Vietnamese fish sauce (also called anchovy sauce) if you can, it is less pungent than the Thai nam pla. This is a good way to use up leftover cooked chicken or turkey, in which case miss out the poaching instructions.

2 boneless, skinless chicken breasts

50g redskin peanuts (with thin skins on)

2 tablespoons sesame seeds

150g firm white cabbage

2 medium carrots

100g swede or ½ jicama (optional)

1 yellow pepper or green mango (optional)

a large handful of a mixture of Thai basil, coriander and mint, roughly torn

3 spring onions, finely sliced

for the dressing

6 tablespoons lime juice

4 tablespoons Vietnamese fish sauce or 3 tablespoons nam pla

3 tablespoons rice vinegar

2 teaspoons raw mild honey

¼–½ red chilli, finely chopped, according to taste

2 garlic cloves, finely chopped or grated

Poach the chicken in a medium saucepan of boiling, salted water for 10–15 minutes or until cooked through. Drain and leave to cool.

Toast the peanuts in a dry pan until they start to blacken in patches. Pour them onto a clean tea-towel to cool. Fold up the towel and massage them with your hands to remove the skins. Pick out the peanuts (don't worry if some skins stay on). Roughly chop them with a knife and set aside. Toast the sesame seeds in a dry pan until they start to pop and brown. Toss frequently, then when golden remove from the heat and tip onto a plate to cool.

Mix the dressing ingredients together in a small bowl.

Finely slice the cabbage with a very sharp knife on a chopping board. Take time to get the shreds very thinly sliced. Tear the chicken into shreds. Cut the carrots, swede and pepper with a sharp knife into julienne strips or use a gadget that shreds. Add them straight into the dressing in a large bowl to prevent them browning.

To assemble the salad mix the chicken, cabbage, peanuts and herbs into the bowl with the remaining ingredients and dressing. Arrange on a serving platter and scatter over the sesame seeds.

variation:
Top with crispy garlic and shallots from the Pomelo Salad (page 158).

fruity salad & korean roasted duck with five-spice marinade

serves 2–4

We ate this tender spicy duck salad at the beautiful Y Thao Garden Restaurant in Hue, Vietnam, and begged the owner for her recipe. I couldn't believe how easy it was but she did say to take care to balance the sweet and sour fruits. If you can't get apricots, use another medium-sweet fruit, such as grapes, peach or plum. Serve with wedges of lime, ready to squeeze into a small dish containing black pepper and salt, and another small dish of pieces of cut pineapple and chilli powder (pages 104–105).

2 boneless and skin-on duck breasts

for the spice rub

1 tablespoon five-spice powder

1 teaspoon caster sugar

½ teaspoon salt

2 small or 1 fat garlic clove, finely chopped

for the dressing

½ quantity of Sesame Ginger Soy Dressing (page 18)

for the fruit salad

seeds of ½ pomegranate

1 firm, unripe kiwi or green mango, peeled and cut into
    0.5cm slices

2 apricots, skin on and thinly sliced

1 hard, unripe avocado, thinly sliced

a large handful of mint leaves, stalks removed, roughly torn

a small handful of tarragon, stalks removed, roughly torn

a small handful of coriander, tough stalks removed, roughly torn

1 lemongrass stalk, very thinly sliced

Put the duck breasts in a shallow dish. Combine the rub ingredients in a small bowl and rub into the duck pieces. Cover and set aside to marinate for up to 1 hour in the fridge.

Remove the duck from the fridge and put into a cold, dry non-stick frying pan, skin-side down. Put over a medium heat and cook for 10 minutes or until the skin has become crispy, turn the breasts over and cook on the other side for 3–5 minutes until firm to the touch. Remove the breasts from the pan and leave to rest on a warm (but not hot) plate in a warm place for 10 minutes.

Mix the fruit salad ingredients together gently, in a large bowl, with the dressing and arrange on a serving plate. Cut the duck into slices, about 5mm thick, leaving the skin on. Serve warm, straight away, on top of the salad.

confit duck, crispy potato & garlic salad

serves 4–6

We love to pick up cans of confit duck when we see them. The French brands are best and perfect for putting by for another day. This salad comes from our good friend Joe Mosse, who lives in Lyon. She whips up this garlicky, unctuous salad to feed her French husband Loic and teenage children when she's short of fresh ingredients and loves to use home-grown herbs. Our advice is to hide the irresistibly crispy potatoes from teenagers once they are cooked or you won't have any left for the salad.

1.2kg can or jar of duck confit, containing 4–6 pieces of duck with fat

1.25kg Charlotte potatoes or large old potatoes, roughly cut into 3cm cubes

2 large sprigs of rosemary

8 garlic cloves, skin on, lightly crushed

250g baby spinach or watercress or a mixture of the two

a very large handful of mixed soft green herbs, such as flat-leaf or curly parsley, tarragon, wild garlic leaves, chives, chervil, thyme leaves

salt and freshly ground black pepper

for the mustard vinaigrette

2 tablespoons red wine vinegar

3 tablespoons extra virgin olive oil

½–1 teaspoon raw mild honey or maple syrup

1 tablespoon Dijon mustard

1 small garlic clove, finely chopped

Preheat the oven to 200°C/gas mark 6.

Plunge the can (before opening it) into a bowl of very hot water for 10 minutes. This will melt the fat and make it easier to remove the duck pieces. Remove the can from the water and open it. Remove the pieces of duck from the fat and lay onto a oven tray skin-side up, reserving the fat for later. Roast for 15–20 minutes or until piping hot and the skin is crispy. Remove the tray from the oven and set aside in a warm place, loosely covered in foil.

Meanwhile, put the potatoes, rosemary and the garlic cloves onto another oven tray with 200ml of the duck fat poured over the top and season with a generous scattering of salt and pepper. Bake for 40–45 minutes or until the potatoes are crispy and browned.

Make the vinaigrette by shaking the ingredients together in a lidded jar.

Remove the potatoes from the oven and pour away most of the fat. Remove the garlic and pop the pearly insides from their jackets into a warm serving bowl, mash and toss with the potatoes. Set aside in a warm place.

Using two forks, pull the duck meat from the bones and cut the skin into shreds. Add this to the potatoes. Add the spinach and herbs, toss through with the vinaigrette. Taste and season again as necessary.

asian rainbow slaw with korean beef in lettuce wraps

serves 4–6

This dish is based on bulgogi, a Korean barbecued beef traditionally made from large pieces of thinly cut topside. Ask your butcher to cut them for you or buy your favourite cut of steak and slice it into strips. Traditionally the beef is wrapped in a lettuce leaf along with side dishes such as boiled rice, chillies and spring onions. If you have made your own Kimchi (page 174) serve this alongside, too. We like it with this rainbow slaw as it's super healthy, crunchy and so moreish.

750g sirloin steak or thinly sliced, almost shaved, topside

1 tablespoon sesame seeds

8–12 leaves of lettuce to serve such as Romaine, Bibb, Butterhead or Napa cabbage, trim any tough or bitter white stalks away

4 spring onions, finely sliced on the diagonal, to serve

for the marinade

6 spring onions, roughly chopped

5 garlic cloves, peeled and trimmed

2cm piece of fresh ginger, peeled and roughly chopped

4 tablespoons soy sauce

2 tablespoons raw mild honey or maple syrup

1 teaspoon toasted sesame oil

¼–½ red chilli, finely chopped, according to taste

for the asian rainbow slaw

50g peanuts

100g red or white cabbage, finely shredded

1 red pepper, cut into julienne strips

1 medium carrot, cut into julienne strips

3 spring onions, cut into julienne strips

8 radishes, finely sliced

1 celery stick, finely sliced

10g coriander, tough stalks removed, roughly chopped

1 quantity of Sesame Ginger Soy Dressing (with peanut butter – page 18)

Cut the steak into strips about 5mm wide and put them into a shallow dish. Put all the marinade ingredients into a food processor and blend until smooth. Pour the marinade over the steak and leave to marinate for at least 1 hour or overnight, covered, in the fridge.

Toast the peanuts in a dry frying pan, over a medium heat, until browned. Remove from the heat and cut roughly with a sharp knife. Set aside to cool.

Toast the sesame seeds for the steak in a dry pan until they pop and lightly brown, toss frequently. Pour onto a plate to cool.

Make the dressing according to the recipe on page 18.

Prepare the slaw by mixing all the ingredients together, toss with a little of the dressing and arrange on a large platter. Serve the remaining dressing on the side so people can dip their parcels into it.

When ready to cook the beef, heat a large frying pan, griddle or a hotplate to fiercely hot. Using tongs or chopsticks lay the beef strips onto the heat and let them cook for 30 seconds–1 minute on each side or to your liking, turning them once. Discard any remaining marinade. Serve straight away, next to the salad with the sesame seeds scattered over and the lettuce leaves and spring onions on the side.

mexican beef salad

serves 6–8

This spicy and crunchy salad can work with leftover cooked beef from a Sunday roast, a boiled beef brisket or a couple of quickly cooked steaks which can be added at the last minute. I prefer a crisp lettuce such as Romaine or Little Gem but really any leaves are a good backdrop to the spicy beef. If you are short of meat, or prefer it without, crumble over some feta at the end and eat this with Guacamole (page 182), The Dip of Joy (page 59) and crisp tortillas or toasted sourdough bread.

for the dressing

juice of ½ lemon or 1 lime

3 tablespoons best extra virgin olive oil

1 garlic clove, finely chopped

½–1 red or green chilli, according to taste, finely sliced

salt and freshly ground black pepper

for the salad

300–500g cooked beef, torn into bite-sized pieces

100g cucumber, peeled, deseeded and cut into 1.5cm cubes

1 large Romaine lettuce or 4 Little Gem lettuce, torn into bite-sized
   pieces

40g radishes, thinly sliced

100g tomatoes, cored, deseeded and cut into bite-sized pieces

1 tablespoon capers, in salt or brine, drained and rinsed thoroughly

1 red or yellow pepper, cut into 1cm strips

a small bunch of coriander or flat-leaf parsley, tough stalks removed
   and roughly chopped

Combine the dressing ingredients in a bowl and adjust the seasoning to your liking.

Mix the salad ingredients together in a bowl and toss with the dressing to combine. Serve straight away.

rare steak tagliata, salsa verde, charred onions, tomato salad

serves 4

Deliciously punchy green sauces have been around for centuries. Herbs can vary between just parsley to combinations of mint and parsley, coriander, tarragon or chervil, so experiment to find your favourite blend. Salsa verde lasts for up to five days in the fridge, use it on hot new potatoes, on roast lamb or with white fish.

We either barbecue the beef and onions over a grill outdoors or use a griddle pan on the hob. We like to use 28-day aged grass-fed sirloin or splash out on a T-bone – make sure it has enough creamy fat attached as this will provide the cooking fat. Look for a well-marbled appearance with plenty of small veins of fat running through the flesh so it won't end up dry. We lay this on a big wooden board at our restaurants surrounded by the Tomato Salad with Sweet and Sour Onion Vinaigrette (page 139), hunks of crusty sourdough and a jug of extra sauce.

for the salsa verde

100ml olive oil

15g flat-leaf parsley, stalks included

15g mint leaves, stalks discarded

1 tablespoon capers, in salt or brine, drained and rinsed thoroughly

5 anchovy fillets in oil, drained

1 tablespoon lemon juice

1 garlic clove

salt and freshly ground black pepper

for the salad

6 fat spring onions or 12 slim ones

2 large handfuls of salad leaves, such as watercress, baby spinach or soft round lettuce, roughly torn

4 radishes, finely sliced

1 tablespoon lemon juice

2 tablespoons extra virgin olive oil

for the steak

4 x 200g sirloin steaks, 2cm thick or 1 x 800g T-bone steak

First prepare the salsa verde by blending all the ingredients together in a food processor. Adjust the seasoning to taste and set aside.

Lightly brush the onions with olive oil and barbecue or griddle for 2–4 minutes until softened and lightly blackened. Set aside in a warm place.

Season the steaks with salt and pepper, don't be shy of these ingredients and massage them into each side evenly. Take your griddle pan or barbecue and get it so hot that you can feel the intense heat on your palm when you put your hand over it and have to withdraw it quickly. Don't cook more than two steaks at a time in the same pan or they will release too much liquid and boil rather than fry. For the T-bone or a thick-cut sirloin, use a pair of tongs to hold it upright onto the hot surface, fat-side down. Sear it for 3–4 minutes so that the fat crispens and weeps. Move it around so that all the fat has contact with the heat.

Now turn the steak to one side and allow 6–8 minutes a side for a T-bone. It will be well browned on the outside but medium rare inside. For a sirloin allow 1½ minutes a side for rare, 2 minutes a side for medium rare and 2½ minutes aside for the medium. Set aside to rest for the same amount of time as you cooked them.

Toss the salad leaves and radishes together with the lemon juice and olive oil, arrange on a big wooden board or in a bowl.

After the steak has rested, cut it into 1cm-thick slices. Scatter over a few salt flakes and serve on the board with the charred onions and salad. Pour a little of the salsa verde over the steak and serve the remainder in a jug.

greek lemon chicken, grain & feta salad with tzatziki

serves 6

Sometimes we feel like a substantial salad that is a meal in itself with all the elements of good food – plenty of greens, crunchy raw pepper and loads of flavour. This is also a great way to use up leftover chicken or turkey. Serve with a tzatziki dressing and tomato salad. This is our friend Anne Hudson's method of preparing the wonderful Greek yogurt and cucumber dip, which she learned to make the local way when living in Greece. You can also enjoy the tzatziki with bread or as a dip for vegetables.

for the tzatziki

125g cucumber, skin left on, coarsely grated

150g thick Greek yogurt

1 small garlic clove, finely grated

1 tablespoon finely chopped dill

2 teaspoons white or red wine vinegar

1–2 tablespoons extra virgin olive oil

salt and freshly ground black pepper

for the salad

200g grains, such as barley, wheatberries, farro, quinoa or brown rice

600ml chicken stock

4 tablespoons extra virgin olive oil

1 medium white onion, finely chopped

3 garlic cloves, finely chopped

¼–½ teaspoon dried chilli flakes or fresh chilli, according to taste

450g cooked chicken or turkey, torn into bite-sized pieces

2 teaspoons dried oregano

zest and juice of 1 lemon

1 red or green pepper, deseeded and roughly chopped

a handful of flat-leaf parsley, tough stems discarded, roughly chopped

75g feta cheese, crumbled

a handful of watercress or baby spinach

1 lemon, cut into wedges, to serve

 If using quinoa or brown rice.

To make the tzatziki, scatter the cucumber with ¼ teaspoon of salt and leave in a sieve to drain for about 30 minutes. Squeeze out the water from the cucumber with your hands but do not rinse it. Mix with the remaining tzatziki ingredients – the oil can make the tzatziki runny, so add less if you want a dip and a little more if you want a dressing. Taste and season as necessary. Keep in the fridge until ready to serve.

Cook the grains in the chicken stock with a little salt according to the packet instructions. Drain and set aside.

Meanwhile, heat the oil in a large frying pan and cook the onion over a medium heat until softened. It should take 7–10 minutes. Add the garlic and chilli and continue to fry for a minute. Add the cooked grains, chicken, oregano, lemon zest and juice and seasoning and stir through to combine. Taste and adjust the seasoning and balance as necessary with salt, pepper and more lemon. Remove from the heat and mix in the pepper and parsley.

Transfer into a serving dish. At this point it can be cooled and refrigerated (within an hour if using rice) and kept for a day. To serve, allow the salad to come to room temperature (unless you have used rice, in which case serve it chilled) and top with crumbled feta and watercress. Serve with the tzatziki and lemon wedges.

salads from the sea

wild rice & herb salad with charred sardines

salmon, asparagus & pea salad with watercress dressing

hot spicy prawns meet cool cucumber salad

crab & celery salad with brown crabmeat fritters

sea bass, cucumber & samphire salad with basil dressing

tuna niçoise with green beans, potatoes & sun-dried tomatoes

japanese salmon salad bowl

japanese-style brown rice

reiko's pickled cucumbers

stir-fried sesame carrots with a hint of chilli

wakame seaweed salad

indian flower salad with zahda's tandoori salmon & prawns

fish tacos with shredded cabbage & coriander salad

poke bowl

wild rice & herb salad with charred sardines

serves 4–6

This is inspired by eating grilled sardines cooked on a boat on the Bosphorus in Istanbul. They were packed into bread with onions, loads of flat-leaf parsley and lemon juice and wrapped in newspaper. We have taken those flavours to make a lemon and herb rice salad to serve with sardines and it's even better with a dollop of homemade Mayonnaise (page 21).

4–6 sardines, filleted and descaled

for the salad

300g wild and brown rice

1 small red onion, finely chopped

2 tablespoons soft thyme leaves

30g flat-leaf parsley leaves, roughly chopped

1 celery stick, plus a handful of celery leaves, finely chopped

3 heaped tablespoons roughly chopped basil

50g can anchovy fillets in oil, drained and roughly chopped

12 green olives stuffed with chilli, halved, or 12 green olives and
   ½ teaspoon dried chilli flakes

for the lemon dressing

4 tablespoons lemon juice (approx. 1 large lemon)

1 teaspoon finely grated lemon zest

8 tablespoons extra virgin olive oil

1 teaspoon Dijon mustard

salt and freshly ground black pepper

Cook the rice in plenty of boiling salted water in a medium saucepan until tender. It should take about 25 minutes. Drain and spread out into a dish to cool quickly. Put it into the fridge within an hour to avoid food poisoning.

Meanwhile, soak the chopped onion in cold water for 10–20 minutes.

Combine all the dressing ingredients in a jug, stir well and season to taste. Put the salad ingredients into a large serving bowl and toss with the dressing. Taste and adjust the seasoning to your preference adding more salt, pepper, chilli and lemon juice if necessary.

Season the sardine fillets on both sides and cook under a hot grill or on a barbecue until cooked through and firm to the touch, turning once during cooking. Serve straight from the grill on top of the salad.

salmon, asparagus & pea salad with watercress dressing

serves 6

This quintessentially English dish of pink poached salmon against a verdant selection of leaves is as vibrant as a sunny spring day. It is easy to put together and the fish and dressing can be prepared in advance, so it's ideal for entertaining.

750g fillet of salmon or 1 side of a small salmon, skin on and
　　pin-boned
2 tablespoons white wine
a small handful of pea shoots
salt and freshly ground black pepper

for the dressing
1 shallot, finely chopped
1 tablespoon extra virgin olive oil
100g watercress
200ml crème fraîche

for the salad
12 asparagus spears, woody ends removed
300g fresh peas
a small handful of dill, stems removed
a small handful of mint leaves, roughly torn
a small handful of tarragon leaves, stems removed
a handful of watercress
½ English cucumber, peeled and thinly sliced
juice of ½ lemon
2 tablespoons extra virgin olive oil

Preheat the oven to 180°C/gas mark 4.

Put the salmon on a large piece of baking parchment, spoon over the wine, season and secure the edges of the parchment to form a parcel, then cook for 20–25 minutes or until just cooked through. Remove from the oven and leave to cool while you prepare the remaining ingredients. When cool enough to touch, remove the skin and flake the fish into large pieces.

Boil or steam the peas and asparagus – about 10 minutes for the peas and 5–8 minutes for the asparagus. Plunge the vegetables into cold water to cool quickly and keep their colour.

Meanwhile, prepare the dressing by frying the shallot in the oil with salt and pepper in a small pan over a gentle heat until softened, but make sure it does not take on any colour. Remove from the heat and leave to cool. Pour this into a food processor, add the watercress and whizz. Add the crème fraîche and pulse until well blended. Season to taste.

Put all the salad vegetables and herbs in a large bowl, toss in the lemon juice and olive oil and arrange around the edge of a platter. Lay the salmon on top, in the centre, and splash on the crème fraîche dressing or serve on the side. Scatter the pea shoots on top of the salmon.

hot spicy prawns meet cool cucumber salad

serves 4

Plump, pink, spicy prawns, soft white noodles and coriander in a lime butter sauce – what's not to like? My brother-in-law Robbo loves to cook this when he comes to stay. He and my sister Carly love Thai flavours but as they live partly in Spain they were inspired by the way the Spanish cook buttery, spicy prawns gambas pil-pil, hence this beautifully decadent combination.

Robbo serves the prawns and peppers with crusty bread to soak up the juices but we add rice noodles for the gluten-free family members. Both ways are just as good.

360g raw tiger prawns, shelled

juice of 2 limes

300g rice noodles (optional)

100g cucumber (approx. 1/3 English cucumber), peeled and cut into ribbons with a peeler or spiraliser

1 red Romano pepper, deseeded and sliced into 1cm wide strips

a handful of coriander leaves, tough stems removed

50g butter

3 tablespoons olive oil

20g fresh ginger, peeled and finely grated

1/2–1 red chilli, according to taste, finely chopped

5 fat garlic cloves, finely grated or chopped

salt and freshly ground black pepper

If there are visible black veins down the back of the prawns, make a shallow cut down their outer curves, using a sharp knife, and hook them out. Discard. If there is nothing visible, leave the prawns intact. Put the prawns in a bowl with the lime juice, season and leave to marinate for 10 minutes.

If using, cook the noodles according to the packet instructions. Rinse under cold water until cool to the touch, drain thoroughly and put into a bowl.

Put the cucumber, pepper and coriander into a large mixing bowl.

Heat the butter and oil in a medium saucepan and when hot add the ginger, chilli and garlic. Cook for a couple of minutes or until you can smell the flavours. Add the prawns and cook for 3–4 minutes until pink. Remove the prawns with a slotted spoon and set aside in a warm bowl.

Now tip the noodles into the pan with the buttery sauce and stir to coat them. Pour these into the bowl with the cucumber and add the prawns. Use a pair of tongs to toss and combine the whole salad, transfer to a large warm platter and serve straight away.

crab & celery salad with brown crabmeat fritters

serves 6

This recipe solves the problem of what to do with the brown meat when buying crab. Spoonfuls of brown crabmeat are frozen and encased in breadcrumbs then fried just before serving. Inside the crabmeat melts and becomes soft and creamy; with a squeeze of lemon they are completely delicious. We like to serve this in vintage Champagne saucers.

for the fritters

100g brown crabmeat

1 egg

4 tablespoons plain or gluten-free flour

4 tablespoons wholemeal or gluten-free fine breadcrumbs

750ml sunflower or nut oil, for frying

for the salad

300g white crabmeat

1 large avocado, peeled, stoned and sliced

1 large celery stick, finely sliced on the diagonal

1 tablespoon celery leaves, finely chopped (optional)

a small handful of flat-leaf parsley leaves, roughly chopped

2 tablespoons lemon juice

4 tablespoons extra virgin olive oil

salt and freshly ground black pepper

lemon wedges and rocket, to serve

For the fritters, squeeze a heaped teaspoonful of brown crabmeat between 2 teaspoons into a quenelle (the size of a quail egg with two pointed ends). Use one spoon to scoop the shape out of the other and lay onto a tray and repeat to use up all the crabmeat – you should have about 12 quenelles. Transfer the tray to the freezer for a couple of hours. This can be done up to 2 days in advance.

Prepare three separate bowls of the coating ingredients; one each for the egg, flour and breadcrumbs. Take the frozen quenelles of brown crabmeat and dip them one at a time into the flour, egg and breadcrumbs to coat. Put them back on the cold tray and refreeze for at least 30 minutes. Work quickly as you want the meat to remain frozen during this process. The fritters are now ready to fry just before serving.

Toss the white crabmeat, avocado, celery and leaves, if using, and parsley in a bowl with the lemon juice and oil. Season to taste. Spoon into serving dishes and keep chilled until you are ready to serve.

Heat the oil in a deep-fat fryer or high-sided pan until hot enough to sizzle a small piece of bread. Remove the fritters from the freezer and lower about 4 into the hot oil. They will only take a minute to lightly brown, then remove with a slotted spoon and drain on kitchen paper. Repeat with the remaining fritters. Serve straight away on the side of the crab salad with a sprinkle of salt, a wedge of lemon and a few rocket leaves.

sea bass, cucumber & samphire salad with basil dressing

serves 4–6

Selin Kiazim is a London-based chef who cooks wonderfully flavourful food based on her Turkish roots.

I love this vibrant green and white salad which balances the soft fish perfectly with a delicate basil dressing and crunchy vegetables. If samphire is hard to come by, use some thin cooked green beans instead. The fish can be cooked in a pan or on a barbecue. The salad is lovely as a first or main course, on its own or with rustic bread, Quinoa Kabsa (page 164) or the Ancient Grain Salad (page 157).

for the basil dressing

a handful of basil, stems discarded

a small handful of flat-leaf parsley, tough stems removed

1 small garlic clove

juice of 1 lemon

3 tablespoons extra virgin olive oil

salt and freshly ground black pepper

for the salad

1 tablespoon extra virgin olive oil

4 x 150g fillets of sea bass fillets, pin-boned and skinned

a big handful of crunchy salad leaves, such as Romaine lettuce mixed with some rocket or watercress

a small handful of flat-leaf parsley, thick stems discarded

150g samphire or rocket, tough stems removed

1 cucumber, peeled, deseeded and cut into strips

For the dressing, put the basil, parsley, garlic, lemon juice, olive oil and seasoning into a blender and whizz until smooth. Set aside.

Pour the olive oil into a large non-stick frying pan and gently heat. Season the sea bass fillets and cook for about 1 minute on each side or until just cooked through. Remove from the heat, put onto a plate and set aside.

Gently break up the fillets into large pieces about 5 x 3cm. Spoon some of the dressing all over the fish and leave for about 20 minutes. Alternatively, you could dress the fish and transfer to the fridge overnight so the flavour really penetrates.

To assemble the salad, put the leaves, parsley, samphire, cucumber and sea bass and remaining dressing into a bowl. Season, give it all a gentle mix and serve.

Shredded Chicken & Cabbage Salad (top left – page 79); Vietnamese Spring Rolls (middle left – page 55); Pineapple, Chilli & Salt (bottom left – page 80); Thai Prawn, Carrot & Coriander Salad (middle – page 54); Pomelo Salad with Coconut Lime Dressing (top right – page 158) and Fruity Salad & Korean-roasted Duck with Five-spice Marinade (bottom right – page 80).

vietnamese

tuna niçoise with green beans, potatoes & sun-dried tomatoes

serves 4–6

This is one of our go-to recipes as we normally have most of the ingredients in the cupboard and beans in the fridge. We far prefer the result from the canned sustainably-caught tuna in water or the wonderful fillets of tuna in olive oil available from Italian delis. Fresh tuna just can't compete with the robust umami flavours of anchovy, sun-dried tomato and olives.

Do choose your olives carefully, our favourite are the purplish-brown Kalamata olives that you pit yourself by bashing them with the flat side of a cook's knife.

300g new potatoes

250g long green beans

4–6 eggs

3 spring onions or 1 small red onion, finely sliced

160g can sustainably caught tuna in water or oil, drained (drained weight 112g) and flaked

1 large celery stick, finely chopped

40g sun-dried tomatoes in oil, drained weight, roughly chopped

12 good-quality olives, pitted and halved

1 tablespoon capers, drained and rinsed

50g can anchovy fillets in oil, drained

1 quantity of Classic Vinaigrette (page 20), to serve

Cook the potatoes whole with skins on in plenty of boiling salted water in a large pan until tender. Drain and leave to cool. Cook the beans in another medium pan of boiling salted water until tender. We boil our beans for about 15–20 minutes, Italian-style, so they are soft and sweet, but do leave them crunchy if you prefer. Drain and leave to cool.

Boil the eggs and as soon as they are hard (8 minutes hard-boil will do it) crack the shells and drop them into cold running water, this will stop the bluish colour appearing around the yolk. Peel and set aside.

When the potatoes are cool cut them in half and put in a large salad bowl. Soak the onions in cold water for about 10 minutes to remove the strength, drain and add to the bowl. Cut the beans in half and add to the bowl with the remaining ingredients, except the eggs.

Toss the dressing with the salad. Halve the eggs and add.

variations and additions
Use quail's eggs rather than hen's eggs. Or add bite-sized pieces of avocado or leaves such as shredded Romaine lettuce, watercress, rocket or baby spinach.

japanese salmon salad bowl

serves 6

'Japanese cooking is all about the mixture of textures – the crisp and sharp edges of the cucumbers are important, as are the wilted, soft carrots, the flaky salmon and the chewy, nutty brown rice', explained our good friend and chef Reiko Hara. The look of the food, she told us, is very important, everything should be cut uniformly. You eat with your eyes first and then you taste.

Reiko showed us some Japanese techniques for making salad. She believes food is not just a way to live, it should enrich your life. We feel the same and have had fun combining some of her recipes with our own to make a selection of salads that we serve together to provide balance in taste and texture.

Our salad bowl is based on a bento box, with the idea of eating small amounts of a variety of different foods. We like to serve the salmon with all or a combination of Japanese-style Brown Rice (opposite), Reiko's Pickled Cucumbers, Stir-Fried Sesame Carrots with a Hint of Chilli and Wakame Seaweed Salad (pages 110–111).

125ml tamari (for a gluten-free option) or soy sauce

125ml sake

2 tablespoons maple sryup

400g salmon fillet, skin on

 If using tamari.

Heat the tamari, sake and maple syrup together in a saucepan until the syrup dissolves. Remove from the heat and pour into a bowl then set aside to cool. Put the salmon fillets into a sealable plastic bag or lidded plastic box and pour in the marinade. Lay the bag in a bowl and put the bowl or box in the fridge for at least 2 hours and up to a day for the flavour to strengthen. Turn the bag or box a couple of times during this time to ensure even distribution of the liquid.

Remove the salmon from the bag and discard the marinade. Pat the salmon dry with kitchen paper. Heat the grill to medium hot. There is no need to add oil. Grill the salmon, skin-side up, until crisp, turn and grill on the other side until cooked through and firm to the touch. Remove from the grill and serve straight away.

japanese-style brown rice

serves 6

Not strictly Japanese but an invention of our son Flavio. He simply stirs soy sauce and finely chopped pickled sushi ginger into the rice. It has sweetness from the pickling juice, savoury from the soy and bite from the ginger.

500g cooked brown rice

1 tablespoon soy sauce or tamari (for a gluten-free option)

2 tablespoons sushi ginger, finely chopped

4 tablespoons sushi ginger pickling juice

1 crisp nori sheet (optional)

 If using tamari.

Stir the rice while still warm or at room temperature with the soy sauce, ginger and juice to taste. Crispen the nori sheet under the grill, if using, and crumble it over the rice to serve.

reiko's pickled cucumbers

serves 6

In a part of any Japanese meal there will always be a vegetable dressed in vinegar. If you can get hold of them use Lebanese cucumbers as they are firmer and have less seeds so there is no need to remove them. If you use English cucumbers, cut the cucumber in half lengthways and remove the seeds with a spoon. Reiko told us it is important to take the water out of the ingredients so the salad doesn't become watery.

150g Lebanese or English cucumber
1½ teaspoons salt, plus extra for rolling the cucumber
100ml Japanese rice vinegar
70g caster sugar

To stop the skin being bitter and to clean it, roll the cucumber in salt on a board. Cut the cucumber lengthways, deseed with a spoon if using English cucumber, and chop into half-moon slices about 5mm thick. Put the slices into a sieve with a light covering of salt and leave to drain.

Put the vinegar, sugar and 1½ teaspoons salt together with 175ml water in a small saucepan and heat to dissolve the sugar. Remove from the heat, pour into a bowl and leave to cool.

Add the cucumber slices and leave them to soak for 10 minutes (no longer or they will become soggy). Remove from the bowl and drain well. Serve straight away or store in the fridge for a couple of days.

stir-fried sesame carrots with a hint of chilli

serves 6

This was developed by our son Flavio who loves carrots and Asian flavours, it is based on a Japanese kinpira carrot and burdock salad. It can be eaten straight away or prepared the day before you need it. You don't have to have it with Japanese food – it is also lovely with grilled meats and has a wonderful background heat and warmth. Reiko uses grapeseed oil as it has no taste.

400g carrots or 300g carrots and 100g parsnips, peeled and
    sliced into ribbons
¼–½ hot red chilli, according to taste, finely chopped
2 tablespoons grapeseed oil
1 teaspoon toasted sesame oil
1 tablespoon tahini
1 tablespoon tamari (for a gluten-free option) or soy sauce
5 chives, very thinly sliced
1 teaspoon black sesame seeds

    If using tamari.

Cook the vegetable ribbons and chilli briefly in the grapeseed oil in a large frying pan or wok, turning them constantly with chopsticks or tongs. They should wilt a little and soften in about 5 minutes.

Mix the sesame oil, tahini and tamari or soy sauce in a small dish and add to the pan with the chives, toss to combine. Serve straight away or at room temperature with the sesame seeds scattered over the top.

wakame seaweed salad

serves 6

Wakame is a type of seaweed readily available in Asian shops and good food stores. Make sure you squeeze the seaweed after rehydrating so that any remaining water doesn't dilute the sauce. Soy sauce is often overused by non-Japanese, it should enhance not overwhelm the flavour of the salad.

10g dried wakame seaweed
2 tablespoons rice vinegar
1 tablespoon tamari (for a gluten-free option) or soy sauce
1 teaspoon finely grated fresh ginger
2 teaspoons raw mild honey
¼–½ hot red chilli, according to taste, finely chopped
1 teaspoon toasted sesame oil
2 spring onions, finely sliced
1 tablespoon toasted sesame seeds

   If using tamari.

Put the wakame into a large bowl and cover with boiling water. Let it stand for about 10 minutes or until it has become green and soft. Drain the wakame, rinse under cold water and leave to drain.

Whisk the vinegar, tamari, ginger, honey, chilli and sesame oil together. Add the wakame along with the spring onions and toss well. Put into a mound on a serving platter or spoon into a serving dish and sprinkle with toasted sesame seeds. Serve straight away.

indian flower salad with zahda's tandoori salmon & prawns

serves 6

This recipe is from the Punjab where cookery teacher Zahda Saeed's family originated. Tandoori chicken is usually made with chicken thighs but works just as well with seafood. If you are using chicken thighs cook them for an extra 10–20 minutes. Zahda often prepares and marinates meat and fish the night before and cooks it the next day. She likes the fact that it is healthy Indian food and serves it with warmed pittas and salad. The yellow egg powder adds a rich orangey red colour to the dish but it can be left out if you prefer, and replaced it with turmeric for a golden colour.

for the fish or meat and marinade

1kg salmon fillet, skin-on and pin-boned

8–10 shell-on tiger prawns or 1.2 kg boneless, skin-on
  chicken thighs

2 teaspoons salt

juice of 1 lemon

100g natural yogurt

6 garlic cloves, grated

¼ teaspoon ajwain or dried sage (optional)

2–3 heaped teaspoons chilli powder, according to taste

2 teaspoons ground cumin

1 tablespoon garam masala

1 teaspoon raw mild honey (optional)

½ teaspoon cumin seeds

¼ teaspoon egg yellow powder or turmeric for colour (optional)

for the Indian flower salad

25g coconut shavings or desiccated coconut

50g cashews

2 large handfuls of sweet and strongly flavoured salad leaves,
  such as soft round lettuce, Little Gem, rocket, mustard, mizuna
  or nasturtium

1 mango, cut into 2cm dice

10 cherry tomatoes, halved

1 avocado, sliced

a large handful of edible flowers, such as nasturtium, blue borage,
  thyme, sage or coriander

for the dressing

4 tablespoons extra virgin olive oil

zest of ½ lime and juice of 1 lime

1 teaspoon clear honey

¼–½ red chilli, according to taste, finely chopped

salt and freshly ground black pepper

Cut the salmon into 5cm cubes. Put the salmon and prawns or chicken into a large bowl with the salt and the lemon juice and toss to combine. Leave for 10 minutes.

Meanwhile, combine the remaining marinade ingredients in a large bowl. Add the fish and prawns or meat to the marinade with any juices from the bowl and leave to marinate, covered, in the fridge for at least 1 hour and up to 12 hours.

Preheat the oven to 200°C/gas mark 6. Space out the pieces of salmon (not the prawns) or chicken onto a rack with a tray underneath to catch the juices. Splash any leftover marinade over the top and cook the salmon for 15–20 minutes or the chicken for 30–35 minutes. Start the chicken skin-side up and turn when crispy to cook the underside. Add the prawns to the salmon for the last 5 minutes or until cooked through.

Meanwhile, toast the coconut and cashews separately on a baking tray in the oven (the coconut is quicker to cook) until lightly browned. Keep an eye on them as they burn easily and will be done in about 5 minutes. This can also be done in a dry frying pan.

Arrange all the salad ingredients, apart from the flowers, onto a serving dish.

Mix the dressing ingredients, altering the seasoning to taste with salt and chilli; drizzle over the salad and scatter the flowers over the top. Serve the salmon and prawns or chicken alongside the salad.

tip

This recipe also works well on a barbecue, in which case the pieces of meat or fish would be threaded onto skewers for easy turning over the coals. Make sure the chicken is cooked through and the juices run clear when pierced with a skewer.

Spicy Tomato Salsa (top left
– page 171); Fish Tacos with
Shredded Cabbage & Coriander
Salad (middle – page 116);
Pineapple & Ginger Salsa
(bottom right – page 188).

fish tacos with shredded cabbage & coriander salad

serves 4–6

In America, fish tacos (see photo on previous pages) are often made with catfish or mahi mahi but any firm white fish such as haddock or cod is good. If you're gentle with it sea bass is delicious, too, and we also use salmon as its flavour stands up to the spice rub. Tacos are mainly made from corn flatbreads called tortillas, they can be soft more like a wrap or crisp, Tex-Mex style. My sister Louise, who lives in the US, showed me how to make this and told me the fish, including crispy bits of skin, should be 'smushed up' after cooking. She uses large Romaine lettuce leaves to parcel up the fish and trimmings but our kids like to use the soft corn tortillas, so we serve both.

This is one of the few occasions when we advocate using garlic powder due to our Atlantan friend Margaret swearing that you couldn't make fish tacos without it. For another couple of side dishes choose the Guacamole (page 182) or the Pineapple & Ginger Salsa (page 188).

for the cabbage salad

300g white or red cabbage, very finely shredded

3 spring onions, thinly sliced, diagonally, into short lengths

2 tablespoons roughly torn coriander leaves

½–1 chilli, according to taste, finely chopped

salt

for the fish

½ teaspoon chipotle chilli powder or smoked hot paprika

1 teaspoon sweet, mild paprika

4 teaspoons ground cumin

2 teaspoons garlic powder

1 teaspoon salt

1kg white fish fillets, such as sea bass, haddock, cod or sea bream, skin on

2 tablespoons extra virgin olive oil

freshly ground black pepper

to serve

8–10 corn tortillas or whole, large lettuce leaves

2 avocados, sliced

2 limes, cut into wedges

a handful of coriander, tough stems discarded

300ml soured cream or Avocado Cream (page 188)

Pico di Gallo (page 188) or Spicy Tomato Salsa (page 171)

To make the cabbage salad, mix the ingredients together in a serving bowl. There is no dressing as it would make the tacos too wet.

Preheat the oven to 180°C/gas mark 4.

Mix the spices and seasoning for the fish together in a small bowl. Lay the fish fillets onto a chopping board and evenly scatter with spice powder on both sides. Use your hand to pat it onto the fish to make sure it sticks and lay the fish onto a non-stick baking tray skin-side down. Spray or drizzle over the olive oil and transfer to the oven. The fish can also be pan-fried in the oil in a non-stick frying pan if you prefer. Depending on the size of the fillets they will take 5–10 minutes to cook through. If pan-frying, turn the fish after the skin becomes crispy. 'Smush' the fish into large flakes just before serving.

Lay the fish, tortillas, sliced avocado drizzled with the juice of 1 lime wedge, remaining lime wedges, salad, coriander and bowls of cream and salsa onto a large board and serve in the middle of the table so that people can make up their own tacos with a little of everything or just how they like it.

poke bowl

serves 4–6

I had never heard of this brilliant Hawaiian combination of flavours before my LA-based nephew Robbie told me I had to include it. He said poke, pronounced 'pokay', is everywhere in downtown LA. Poke means to cut or slice and it refers to the way the tuna is cut so that it soaks up the dressing quickly. He eats it in bowl form when it is often combined with hot rice, avocado and salad.

It is actually pretty quick to prepare but it is crucial to find sashimi-grade tuna or previously commercially frozen tuna, as it is eaten raw. Keep the rice plain, season with rice vinegar (which is mild and lightly sweet) or serve it our son Flavio's way, see page 108, mixed with chopped sushi ginger and tamari.

for the dressing

1–2 teaspoons wasabi paste, according to taste

juice of 1 lime

2 tablespoons tamari (for a gluten-free option) or soy sauce

1 teaspoon sesame oil

½ teaspoon finely grated fresh ginger

for the tuna and salad

450g very fresh lean yellowfin tuna, cut into 1.5cm dice

3 spring onions, finely chopped

a small handful of fresh coriander, tough stems removed

300g wholegrain long or basmati rice

2 tablespoons rice vinegar

1 avocado, cut into 1.5cm dice

1 tablespoon toasted black or white sesame seeds

¼–½ red chilli, according to taste, very finely diced

salt

Combine the wasabi, lime juice, tamari, oil and ginger in a bowl. Adjust the flavours to suit your taste, it should have bite from the wasabi and sourness from the lime. It won't look like a lot but it is just to coat the fish and avocado, not to swamp it. Put the dressing in the fridge.

Combine the tuna, onions and coriander and set aside in the fridge.

Cook the rice according to the packet instructions. Drain, toss with the vinegar and season with salt.

Now toss the dressing into the fish with the avocado and gently stir to combine. Spoon the rice into bowls and top with the fish mixture. Scatter with sesame seeds and chilli and serve straight away.

  If using tamari.

5

salads from the garden

roast beetroot, lentil & goat's curd salad with walnuts

asparagus with roasted tomato dressing & baked lemon ricotta

pan-fried halloumi & roast florence fennel salad with orange dressing

roast pumpkin, broccoli & bacon salad with mustard dressing

roasted vegetable & orzo pasta salad with basil, pine nuts & parmesan

beetroot patties & beetroot leaf & cress salad with avocado & yogurt dressing

courgette & courgette flower carpaccio with ricotta

portobello mushroom & celery salad with black garlic sourdough crumbs

rubbed kale, butternut squash & farro salad

kale salad with date vinaigrette & sour cherries

green beans with almond & ginger butter

tomato salad with sweet & sour onion vinaigrette

foraged salad with flowers

ginger, sesame & prawn noodle salad jar

mexican quinoa, feta & corn salad jar

falafel salad with hummus

charred broccolini with lemon dressing, capers & pumpkin seeds

shredded carrot, parsley & lemon salad

atsuko's soba noodle salad with sesame dressing

jeremy's silken tofu with chinese chives & toban jiang sauce

roast beetroot, lentil & goat's curd salad with walnuts

serves 4

We grow beetroots and love to use them in this salad. Their flavour concentrates and sweetens with roasting but it takes ages if you leave them whole. By cutting them and partially steaming them in the oven under foil you can reduce the cooking time significantly. We use canned lentils but do cook them from scratch if you prefer.

Soft goat's curd has a delicate flavour. It is wonderful in savoury or sweet dishes, especially when its sour note complements something sweet such as the honey in the dressing.

5 raw medium beetroots

4 tablespoons extra virgin olive oil, plus extra for drizzling

50g walnut halves

1 red onion, cut into 8 wedges

1 x 400g can cooked Puy or beluga lentils (240g drained weight)

1 celery stick, finely sliced on the diagnoal, plus a few leaves

a large handful of flat-leaf parsley, tough stems discarded, roughly chopped, plus extra to garnish

100g goat's curd, soft goat's cheese or feta cheese

salt and freshly ground black pepper

for the dressing

3 tablespoons extra virgin olive oil

1 tablespoon balsamic vinegar

1 teaspoon raw mild honey

Preheat the oven to 200°C/gas mark 6.

Peel and cut the beetroots into wedges about 2cm across at their thickest. Toss with 2 tablespoons of oil and seasoning in a bowl and then tip onto a small oven tray (keep the bowl for the onion). Cover with foil and bake for 30 minutes.

Put the walnuts onto a baking tray and bake for 6 minutes or until lightly roasted and browned. Remove and set aside to cool.

Put the onion in the bowl and toss with 2 tablespoons of oil to coat. Set aside.

When the beetroot has had 30 minutes of cooking, remove the foil and add the onions to the tray, tossing them with the beets. Return to the oven, uncovered, for 20–30 minutes until softened and lightly browned. Remove from the oven and leave to cool on a plate.

Put the lentils into a bowl, add the dressing ingredients and seasoning and toss through. When the beetroots and onions are done, add these and any cooking juices to the lentils and toss together, leave to cool to room temperature.

Stir in the celery and parsley, spoon over the curd or crumble the cheese on top and serve with a little extra parsley, olive oil and freshly ground black pepper.

asparagus with roasted tomato dressing & baked lemon ricotta

serves 4

This couldn't be easier to make and keeps well for a few days in the fridge so is good for entertaining. The dressing also pairs well with grilled fish, lamb, chicken breast or pan-fried goat's cheese. The soft herb and cheese moulds are wonderful with roast asparagus, however when it is not in season serve them with buttered toast, grilled courgettes, roasted and peeled red peppers or heirloom tomatoes.

for the moulds and asparagus

butter, for greasing

250g ricotta, drained

1 egg

a small handful of fresh thyme leaves, finely chopped, plus extra to garnish

25g Parmesan cheese

finely grated zest of ½ unwaxed lemon

250g asparagus, woody ends removed

3 tablespoons extra virgin olive oil

a squeeze of lemon juice

salt and freshly ground black pepper

for the dressing

400g cherry tomatoes

3 tablespoons extra virgin olive oil

a little finely chopped red chilli or finely grated lemon zest, according to taste (optional)

a handful of flaked almonds, toasted, to serve (optional)

Preheat the oven to 180°C/gas mark 4. Generously grease 4 dariole moulds (about 8cm across x 5cm deep) or ramekins with butter and line the bases with baking parchment.

To make the dressing, roast the whole tomatoes on a baking tray for 20–30 minutes or until they have collapsed but not browned. Remove from the oven and leave to cool. Reserve a handful of cherry tomatoes. Tip the remainder into a blender or food processor and blend until smooth. Add the olive oil, salt to taste, and either a little chilli or lemon zest, if you like. The dressing will keep in the fridge, covered, for up to a week.

Make sure the ricotta is well drained. You can do this in a fine sieve or by holding the ricotta in its container over the sink and tipping it. Tip the ricotta into a mixing bowl and stir in the egg, thyme, Parmesan, lemon zest, salt and pepper. Spoon into the moulds and bake for 30–40 minutes or until the tops are lightly golden and firm to the touch. Meanwhile, place the asparagus on a baking tray, season and drizzle with the oil, roast for 15–20 minutes or until tender. Toast the flaked almonds, if using, on a baking tray until lightly browned, they will take 3–5 minutes.

Turn out the moulds and serve straight away or at room temperature, with the asparagus drizzled with the cooking juices and a squeeze of lemon juice, the dressing and a few roasted cherry tomatoes. Garnish with a few toasted almonds and thyme leaves.

pan-fried halloumi & roast florence fennel salad with orange dressing

serves 4–6

Giancarlo learned how to make this punchy orange dressing in Bistrot de Venise restaurant in Venice and now we use it all the time. Reducing the orange juice makes it zing with colour and sweetness. The dressing can be made in advance but fry the halloumi just before serving.

2 fennel bulbs (about 400g total weight), cut into 1cm thick slices

2 tablespoons extra virgin olive oil

a large handful of watercress, rocket or lettuce leaves

a handful of seedless green or red grapes, halved

250g halloumi cheese, cut into 0.5cm slices

a few fronds of wild fennel or dill, stems discarded

salt and freshly ground black pepper

for the dressing

1 teaspoon finely grated orange zest

100ml freshly squeezed orange juice (approx. 2 small oranges)

3 tablespoons extra virgin olive oil

Preheat the oven to 180°C/gas mark 4.

Bring a medium saucepan of water to the boil. Add the fennel slices and boil for 5–10 minutes or until just tender, and drain.

Lay the slices onto a baking tray and brush with the oil and season. Roast for 20–30 minutes or until they start to burn. Little crispy areas are good. Remove from the oven and set aside to cool.

Meanwhile, put the orange zest and juice in a small frying pan over a medium heat, leave it to bubble gently until reduced by about half. Leave to cool. When cool, mix with the oil, salt and pepper. Taste and adjust the seasoning as necessary.

Lay the leaves on a large platter, top with the fennel and grapes.

Dry-fry the halloumi slices, in a non-stick frying pan, on each side for a couple of minutes or until just golden, and add to the salad. Drizzle over the dressing, season with black pepper and scatter over the fennel or dill fronds. Serve straight away or the halloumi will harden.

roast pumpkin, broccoli & bacon salad with mustard dressing

serves 6

Inspired by my nephew Jamie Ford's way of roasting everything on one tray, the contents of this salad simply moved from the fridge to the oven. It makes a perfect entertaining salad for colder autumn days. It contains all the food groups and makes a great meal on its own or as an accompaniment to sausages for supper, all the cooking being done in the oven.

600g pumpkin, sweet potatoes, eddo (taro) or butternut squash, cut into thick wedges, 4cm at widest

5 tablespoons extra virgin or rapeseed olive oil

1 head of broccoli (about 300g), cut into florets

6 rashers of streaky bacon, cut into 2cm strips

2 tablespoons pumpkin seeds

1 quantity of Honey Mustard Dressing (page 19)

75g mature Cheddar or Parmesan cheese, shaved

a small handful of rocket

salt and freshly ground black pepper

Preheat the oven to 180°C/gas mark 4.

Put the pumpkin wedges in a bowl with 3 tablespoons of the oil and seasoning. Toss to combine and then spread out onto a baking tray. Bake for 30 minutes or until soft. After 15 minutes add the broccoli, tossed in seasoning and the remaining oil, and bacon to the tray. Continue to cook until the vegetables and bacon have just started to crispen and brown.

Put the pumpkin seeds onto another small tray and roast for 5 minutes or until they start to pop. Remove everything from the oven and tip into a serving bowl. Pour over the dressing and toss to coat, taste and adjust the seasoning as necessary and top with the shavings of cheese and the rocket. Serve warm.

Fattoush (left – page 161); Spiced
Green Beans with Tomatoes
(top middle – page 162); Quinoa
Kabsa with Nut Hashu (middle
– page 164); Jewelled Beetroot,
Orange, Almond & Dill Salad
(bottom middle – page 176);
Moroccan Crushed Aubergine &
Tomato (right – page 159).

middle eastern

roasted vegetable & orzo pasta salad with basil, pine nuts & parmesan

serves 10

This simple but pretty pasta salad blends well with grilled meat or fish or fills up hungry teenagers all on its own. Other vegetables can be used, such as broccoli, fennel and aubergines. Roast the vegetables in the oven or use a griddle pan or barbecue to give a lightly charred flavour and grill lines. This makes quite a large amount as I often make it for entertaining but it soon gets eaten and keeps well in the fridge overnight.

500g courgettes, cut into 1cm slices

2 red or yellow peppers, deseeded and cut into 1cm wide strips

2 red onions, each cut into 8 wedges

20 cherry tomatoes

7 tablespoons extra virgin olive oil

2 teaspoons dried oregano

6 garlic cloves, left whole with skin on and lightly squashed

a few sprigs of thyme

50g pine nuts

500g orzo

30g Parmesan, finely grated

30g basil leaves, roughly torn, plus a few extra to garnish

salt and freshly ground black pepper

Preheat the oven to 180°C/gas mark 4. Toss the vegetables in a large bowl with 4 tablespoons of the olive oil, the oregano and plenty of pepper and salt and transfer to a roasting tin with the garlic and thyme. Cook for 25–30 minutes or until the vegetables have softened and just starting to brown.

Roast the pine nuts on a baking tray for 3–5 minutes. Remove from the tray and leave to cool.

Meanwhile, cook the orzo according to the packet instructions. Drain and toss with the remaining olive oil in a large serving bowl. Set aside.

Remove the vegetables from the oven and toss through the pasta while still warm. Set aside to cool to room temperature or finish and serve while warm.

Add the remaining ingredients, season well to taste and serve garnished with the extra basil leaves.

beetroot patties & beetroot leaf & cress salad with avocado & yogurt dressing

Makes 10 patties approx. 8cm across x 2cm thick

You can enjoy these knowing that as well as being really tasty they are full of healthy ingredients. Beetroot is packed with vitamins and minerals and loaded with powerful antioxidants. It can help reduce blood pressure, increase stamina and may help to fight heart disease. The leaves are good to eat, too, and even better for you. Cook them as you would spinach and use young leaves raw. Turmeric contains compounds called curcuminoids, which are strong antioxidants. It is good for soothing inflammation. Sesame seeds are an important source of omega-6 fatty acids, flavonoid antioxidants and vitamins. And avocados are packed with vitamins and are very high in potassium, which is linked to lowering blood pressure. They are also thought to help lower cholesterol and their high-fibre content helps to reduce blood sugar spikes.

for the patties

50g oats

150g raw beetroot, coarsely grated

1 medium apple, peeled and coarsely grated

100g feta cheese, coarsely grated

2 spring onions, very finely chopped

1 large egg

2 teaspoons ground cumin

1 teaspoon ground turmeric

50–75g sesame seeds, for coating

salt and freshly ground black pepper

for the avocado and yogurt dressing

1 fat, large, ripe avocado, peeled, stoned and roughly chopped

8 tablespoons live Greek yogurt

1 small garlic clove

¼–½ red chilli, according to taste

juice of ½ lemon

for the salad

a large handful of beetroot leaves or similar, such as mustard or rocket

a large handful of sprouted seeds, such as radish, amaranth, lentils, coriander or cress

2 tablespoons extra virgin olive oil

1 tablespoon lemon juice or splash of vinegar

Preheat the oven to 200°C/gas mark 6. Line a baking tray with baking parchment.

For the patties, whizz the oats in a food processor until they resemble sand. In a large bowl, mix the whizzed oats and all the patty ingredients, except the sesame seeds, together with a large spatula until well blended. Form the mixture into 10 round patty shapes about 8cm across and 2cm deep by squeezing and pressing it together between your palms. They will feel wet but don't worry – it helps to keep them moist during baking.

Pour the sesame seeds into a bowl and completely coat each patty. Place on the lined tray. Bake for about 20 minutes until firm to the touch and lightly golden.

Make the dressing by whizzing the ingredients together in a blender until smooth and glossy. Taste and adjust with seasoning or more chilli and lemon juice to your liking. Set aside in the fridge.

Combine the salad leaves and sprouted seeds and dress just before serving with the olive oil, lemon juice and seasoning. Serve the patties warm or at room temperature with the salad and avocado and yogurt dressing.

Wrap any leftover patties in clingfilm and store in the fridge for about 3 days. The dressing, too, will keep, covered, in the fridge for up to 3 days.

courgette & courgette flower carpaccio with ricotta

serves 4–6

This is light and lovely with a delicious floral sweetness from the melon. To make the salad even prettier, tear a few bright yellow courgette flowers into the salad if you have them. We have a small melon baller to make the pearls but if you don't have one simply cut the melon into small cubes instead.

for the dressing

½–1 red or green chilli, according to taste, finely chopped

1 small garlic clove, finely grated

finely grated zest of ½ lemon, plus extra to garnish

2 tablespoons extra virgin olive oil

salt and freshly ground black pepper

for the salad

3 medium courgettes, thinly sliced

4 round tomatoes, diced or 8 cherry tomatoes, halved

1 red pepper, deseeded and finely sliced

a handful of basil leaves, tough stems discarded

½ honeydew or cantaloupe melon (about 150g flesh), cut into pearls

100g ricotta, drained

Mix the dressing ingredients together in a bowl. Season to taste and set aside.

Arrange a layer of courgette slices, tomatoes and red pepper strips onto one large serving plate or individual ones. Pour over a little dressing. Add the remaining sliced vegetables on top followed by the remaining dressing. (At this point the salad will keep for a few hours in the fridge if you want to serve it later.)

Just before serving, scatter over the basil leaves and melon pearls and top with teaspoon-sized quenelles of ricotta. To do this squeeze a heaped dessertspoonful of ricotta between 2 dessertspoons into a quenelle, an egg shape with pointed ends. Use one spoon to scoop the shape out from the other and lay onto the salad. Grate a little extra lemon zest on top and finish with a good twist of black pepper.

portobello mushroom & celery salad with black garlic sourdough crumbs

serves 4

This dramatic dark salad is perfect for cool nights. It is a fabulous vegan main course or a substantial starter for dinner. Addictively gorgeous black garlic can be found online or in delis. It is not strong like fresh garlic but has a deeply savoury and umami flavour achieved by exposing whole bulbs to low heat and humidity over a period of weeks. Treat yourself to a pot and use it spread onto hot toast or minced into a salad dressing. If you can't get hold of black garlic use regular garlic instead.

for the salad

50g stale sourdough bread

2 tablespoons thyme leaves

5 tablespoons extra virgin olive oil, plus 2 tablespoons for brushing

6 medium black garlic cloves, roughly chopped or 1 fat garlic clove, finely chopped

4 large portobello mushrooms (about 300g total weight)

a large handful of red salad leaves, such as mustard, beetroot or radicchio

1 celery stick, finely sliced on the diagonal

a handful of celery leaves, torn

salt and freshly ground black pepper

for the red wine dressing

200ml good-quality red wine

5 tablespoons extra virgin olive oil

2 teaspoons lemon juice

2 teaspoons raw mild honey or maple syrup (for a vegan option)

Preheat the oven to 200°C/gas mark 6. Line a baking tray with baking parchment.

Tear the bread into small shreds about 2cm in size. Put in a bowl and toss with the thyme, oil, garlic and seasoning. Spread out onto the lined tray and cook for 5–7 minutes or until they become crisp. Tip the bread chunks onto a plate to cool. Heat the grill to high.

Remove any woody parts from the end of the mushroom stems. Turn the mushrooms with the stems facing down and brush with half the oil. Grill them on a rack for 10 minutes or until softened and wrinkled around the edges. Surplus water will ooze out of them so do have a tray underneath to catch the drops. Turn them stem upwards, brush with the remaining oil and season and grill again until lightly crisp around the outer edge and cooked through. Remove from the grill and keep warm.

To make the dressing, put the wine in a small pan, bring to the boil and reduce to one-third of the original volume, about 60ml. Remove from the heat and pour into a jug with the remaining ingredients and whisk vigorously to combine. Season to taste and set aside to cool.

Mix the salad leaves, celery and celery leaves with a little dressing.

Put the mushrooms onto a plate and splash a little of the dressing over the top. Pile the salad next to them followed by the bread chunks and serve with any extra dressing on the side.

rubbed kale, butternut squash & farro salad

serves 6

This very simple warm salad is a lovely meal on its own or with cheese sauce splashed over the top or with fried eggs. Alternatively, serve it as an accompaniment to sausages or roasted meat. Brown or red rice or quinoa can be used instead of farro. This is the only pre-cut vegetable we would buy; our local supermarket does a bag of mixed squash and sweet potato slices which makes life very easy.

200g farro

350g mixed butternut squash and sweet potato thin wedges, approx. 1cm at the widest edge, peeled

2 red onions, peeled and each cut into 8 wedges

3 garlic cloves, skins on and lightly crushed with the flat of a knife

4 tablespoons extra virgin olive oil, plus extra for the kale

a handful of baby kale, or large leaves, shredded or baby spinach leaves

salt and freshly ground black pepper

Preheat the oven to 200°C/gas mark 6. Line a baking tray with baking parchment.

Cook the farro according to the packet instructions in salted water. When tender, drain and set aside.

Put the squash, potato, onions and garlic onto the lined tray, season and drizzle with oil. Toss to coat evenly. Roast for 25–30 minutes until golden brown. Remove from the oven and toss with the farro in a large, warm, serving bowl. Squeeze the roasted garlic cloves out and mix into the salad. Taste and adjust the seasoning as necessary.

If using kale, massage it with your hands for a couple of minutes with a little oil and salt until it softens and brightens in colour. Alternatively, stir a few spinach leaves into the salad. Serve the salad warm.

variation: rubbed kale & cranberries

Kale is best broken down a little if you are going to eat it raw. Pull away the tough stems from the centre of the kale leaves. You can do this by pulling your fingers down the central rib and separating it from the leaves. This can be chopped and boiled or discarded. Tear the leaves into bite-sized pieces and put into a large bowl with the juice of ½ lemon, 1 tablespoon of extra virgin olive oil and ¼ teaspoon of sea salt for each large handful of leaves. Now, firmly massage the leaves with the juices for 3–4 minutes. They will brighten in colour and soften in texture. Serve them as they are or add a handful of cranberries or other dried fruit for sweetness and 1 tablespoon of toasted sesame seeds for some crunch.

kale salad with date vinaigrette & sour cherries

serves 4–6

We have to admit to thinking that sometimes eating a whole bowl of kale feels like a penance. However, a recent visit to The Butcher's Daughter in New York changed that and inspired this recipe. Their kale salad is deliciously sweet with dates and cherries and crunchy with sunflower seeds. The ripped-up kale was easy to eat and we would regularly go back for more if we weren't a couple of thousand miles away. Try to find dried cherries or cranberries with no added sugar and oil. Good delis sell them or find them online, some are loaded with sugar and we prefer to have the natural sourness of an unadulterated dried fruit.

for the vinaigrette

3 Medjool dates, pitted

3 tablespoons balsamic vinegar

4 tablespoons extra virgin olive oil

salt and freshly ground black pepper

for the salad

30g flaked almonds

250g cavolo nero (black or lacinato kale), washed, shredded and drained

30g sunflower or pumpkin seeds, toasted

25g dried sour cherries or cranberries

Preheat the oven to 180°C/gas mark 4.

Whizz together the dressing ingredients in a blender until smooth. Adjust the seasoning as necessary.

Toast the flaked almonds on a baking tray for 3–5 minutes until lightly browned. Remove from the tray and leave to cool. Break them up a little with your hands.

Put the salad ingredients in a large bowl and mix the dressing in. Use a pair of tongs to toss the kale until it is coated in the dressing. Transfer to a serving dish and eat straight away or leave, covered, in the fridge for up to 2 hours.

green beans with almond & ginger butter

serves 4–6

We love almond butter and after experimenting with it one day, we came up with this simple recipe to change an ordinary vegetable into something really moreish with an Asian flavour. We like this salad just as it is but you could scatter toasted sesame seeds or crushed toasted almonds over the top. We sit down to a bowl of this for a quick lunch on its own or pair it with other Asian dishes or grilled meats.

250–300g long green or runner beans, trimmed as necessary

2 tablespoons almond, cashew or peanut butter

1 garlic clove, finely grated

4cm piece of fresh ginger, finely grated

sea salt flakes

a small handful of crushed toasted almonds or 1 tablespoon toasted sesame seeds (optional)

Boil or steam the beans until tender. We prefer them slightly soft after about 10 minutes cooking but if you like them crunchy, give them about 5 minutes.

Meanwhile, mix the nut butter with the remaining ingredients and 2 tablespoons of water to form a soupy paste. When the beans are done drain them well then mix with the dressing in a serving bowl. Serve warm or leave to cool to room temperature, then scatter with the salt and nuts or seeds, if using.

tomato salad with sweet & sour onion vinaigrette

serves 6

This recipe began with an intriguing and moreish tomato and shallot salad at the wonderful Fat Radish restaurant in New York. Perfectly ripe heirloom tomatoes were dressed with what looked like oil and there wasn't an onion in sight. Yet the flavour of the tomatoes had all the caramel notes of roasted onions. At this time we were also given an Italian Jewish recipe by Silvia Nacamulli for sweet and sour onions. The cooking juices from the onions had the exact flavour we were looking for, so here we have the best of both recipes; a rich and unctuous onion vinaigrette for a tomato salad and caramelised onions to be eaten as antipasti on cocktail sticks with rough nuggets of mature cheese.

for the onions & vinaigrette

500g pickling onions

100ml extra virgin olive oil

3 tablespoons cider or white wine vinegar

3 tablespoons Marsala or sweet wine

2–3 teaspoons raw mild honey or maple syrup (optional)

salt

for the salad

1kg perfectly ripe heirloom tomatoes

a few leaves of purslane, nasturtium leaves or baby spinach

a few leaves of purple or regular basil

Maldon sea salt and freshly ground black pepper

     If using maple syrup.

Soak the onions in lukewarm water for 5 minutes before peeling them. Cut only the very ends of the woody roots away from the onions but keep them intact so the layers stay together. Warm the olive oil in a heavy-based saucepan and add the onions with a pinch of salt. Cook over a high heat for a couple of minutes until they turn golden. Reduce the heat and add 2 tablespoons of warm water, the vinegar, Marsala and the honey or maple syrup, if using. Cover with a lid and simmer for 20–30 minutes, stirring occasionally, until the onions are just soft and caramelised. Leave to cool. Drain and reserve the onions and a little of their juice to serve as antipasti. Reserve the remaining juices for the tomato salad.

Cut the tomatoes into wedges and arrange on a large plate or in a shallow bowl, then toss with the onion cooking juices – you may not need all of it but it keeps well in the fridge for another day. Add the leaves and herbs and finish with a little Maldon sea salt and a twist of pepper.

foraged salad with flowers

serves 4–6

Way back in the 15th century, Italian writer and gardener Castelvetro reprimanded the English for eating too much meat and not enough vegetables and salad. He pointed out the plants, flowers and wild herbs that were growing around us that we simply ignored. He described a spring mixed salad as 'the best and most wonderful of all. Take young leaves of mint, those of garden cress, basil, lemon balm, the tips of salad burnet, tarragon, swine cress, the young shoots of fennel, leaves of rocket, of sorrel, rosemary flowers, some sweet violets and the tenderest leaves or the heart of lettuce.'

Centuries later, we are still not that good at variety in most green salads. I have been gathering wild garlic, early spring nettles and feathery wild fennel for years but I recently attended a foraging course with John Rensten from Forage London. As John says, 'a salad should be like an interesting conversation, a spicy flower like the nasturtium or a leaf of wild chicory adding a punchy note against a base of pleasant green.'

Adding a variety of herbs and wild plants will make your salad individual and will depend entirely on what you found that morning, what season you are in and where you are in the world. Our mix from one rainy spring day was dandelion, violets, borage, jack in the hedge, rocket, plantain, sweet cecily, primrose and nasturtium, but you could equally add Castelvetro's suggestions above or sage flowers, parsley, dill, marigolds, edible daisies, mint, fat hen, wild chicory, rocket, chive and chive flowers to a base of lettuce.

We love good eggs with this salad but it also goes well with roast chicken, goat's cheese or a handful of toasted pumpkin seeds.

for the salad
150g mixed leaves (see introduction)
1 garlic clove, halved

for the dressing
4 tablespoons rapeseed oil
1 tablespoon cider vinegar
4 teaspoons wholegrain mustard
2 teaspoons raw mild honey
salt and freshly ground black pepper
edible flowers (see introduction), to garnish

Wash and dry the leaves (see page 10). Wipe a large serving dish with the garlic clove to give the salad a gentle flavour.

Whisking the dressing ingredients together in a large bowl. Taste and adjust the seasoning to get a balance of sweet and sour. Roughly tear the leaves on top and toss with the dressing. Arrange in the garlicky dish with the flowers on top.

salad in a jar

Whatever did we do before someone thought of putting salad in a jar to take to work? While some are still happy to use an old ice-cream container with a dodgy-fitting lid to hide their soggy sandwiches, others have taken to the more stylish packed lunch in a Mason jar, the contents of which are on display for all to see.

Salad in a jar should be built in layers and you should make sure it won't be tipped up before you get to work. If you combine all the food groups you won't be searching for a cake at tea time. So make sure you have protein, starchy pulses or grains, vegetables and fruit as well as salad leaves in your jar. Incidentally, jar salads are not just for work, they are great for entertaining as they can be prepared in advance and handed round with long spoons – they even work at buffets when guests are not sitting down.

Start with the dressing on the bottom. Move up to moisture-resistant vegetables, such as carrots, cucumber or beans and pulses. Then add a layer of veggies such as grated carrot, fruit or cabbage followed by protein such as chicken, cheese, chickpeas, nuts, quinoa or farro. Follow this with berries such as blueberries or strawberries or tomatoes that might break at the bottom, and finish with the most delicate layer, such as herbs and leaves, crumbly bacon or breadcrumbs and screw on the lid. *Et voilà*, your healthy lunch is done and ready to go. Simply keep it in the work fridge until lunch. When ready to eat, turn upside down and shake to mix the dressing with the salad. Eat with a spoon or fork or tip it onto a plate, allowing the dressing to fall evenly over the salad.

ginger, sesame & prawn noodle salad jar

makes enough for 2 x 0.5–0.75-litre wide-mouthed jars

You may want to omit the onions depending upon how you feel about breathing on your colleagues later! Alternatively, soak the onions in cold water for 15–30 minutes to reduce their strength. The salad will keep for 2 days in the fridge so you could prepare it one evening and enjoy it for the next 2 days.

100g rice noodles

1 tablespoon flavourless oil, such as groundnut or grapeseed

2 tablespoons peanuts or cashews

6 tablespoons Sesame Ginger Soy Dressing or Korean Sesame Yogurt Sauce (page 18)

½–¼ red or green hot chilli, according to taste (optional)

1 medium carrot, coarsely grated

½ red pepper, deseeded, finely sliced and cut into bite-sized pieces

2 spring onions, finely sliced (optional)

150g cooked, peeled prawns

a small handful of salad leaves

a small handful of coriander leaves

  If using tamari in the Sesame Ginger Soy Dressing.

Cook the rice noodles according to the packet instructions. When tender, drain and rinse in cold water. Drain well and toss with the oil so that they don't stick together. Set aside.

Dry-fry the nuts over a medium heat until browned. Remove from the heat and leave to cool. Cut roughly with a sharp knife.

Divide the dressing between two jars and stir in the chilli, if using. Top with carrot and red pepper followed by the spring onions, if using. Add a layer of prawns followed by the noodles and then the leaves. Finish with the toasted nuts and close the lids. The salads are done, keep cool until ready to eat.

mexican quinoa, feta & corn salad jar

makes enough for 2 x 0.5–0.75-litre wide-mouthed jars

The heavenly combination of sweet kernels of corn and salty crumbled feta eaten in Pulqueria, a Mexican restaurant in New York, was the inspiration for this salad. It was served in a jar with a long spoon and after a couple of margaritas our minds wandered onto what else would fit in a jar and balance on a spoon without dropping onto your lap at work. Grains are an obvious bet, so are cherry tomatoes and the combination of lime juice and coriander generally just makes life better. If you have fresh cobs of corn, boil them until cooked, scrape off the kernels and use instead of the canned variety. If you have any leftover Ancient Grain salad (page 157), use this or simply boil up some quinoa. The salad will keep for 2 days in the fridge so you can prepare it one evening and enjoy it for the next 2 days.

80g quinoa

2 tablespoons lime juice

6 tablespoons best olive oil

120g canned or fresh, cooked sweetcorn

80g feta cheese, crumbled

a few whole cherry tomatoes

a handful of salad leaves

a small handful of fresh coriander, roughly torn

salt and freshly ground black pepper

Cook the quinoa according to the packet instructions. Set aside to cool.

Divide the lime juice and olive oil between each jar, add the seasoning and swirl together. Top with the sweetcorn and feta to form a barrier against the dressing followed by a layer of the cooked, seasoned quinoa. Top with the tomatoes, a small handful of salad leaves mixed with the coriander and screw on the lids. The salads are ready to go. Keep cool until ready to eat.

indian

Papi & Ranjit's Cabbage & Carrot Salad with Peas (top left – page 175); Fresh Mango Chutney (middle left – page 188); Roasted Cauliflower in Garam Masala with Mango Yogurt Dressing (bottom left – page 48); Nepalese Spicy Onion & Potato Salad (middle – page 172); Cucumber Raita (far right – page185) .

falafel salad with hummus

makes about 20 patties

This recipe for typical Jewish falafel was given to us by Silvia Nacamulli who teaches Jewish cookery. Silvia told me to use dried chickpeas and soak them overnight, as canned chickpeas become soggy and won't hold together while cooking. We like the falafel coated in crunchy sesame seeds.

This is our Kuwaiti friend Amal's hummus recipe; she likes to make it silky smooth but if you prefer a little crunch stop whizzing before it becomes smooth. Hummus keeps well in the fridge for up 4 days, covered, so you have it to hand for serving with toasted pitta bread, on salads or toast for breakfast.

for the falafel

250g dried chickpeas, soaked overnight in cold water

1 small onion, roughly chopped

1 tablespoon sweet, mild paprika

2 teaspoons ground cumin

3 garlic cloves, crushed

a small handful of flat-leaf parsley, tough stalks discarded

a large handful of fresh coriander, tough stalks discarded

¾–1 teaspoon salt

1 tablespoon sesame seeds or toasted sesame seeds

3–4 tablespoons sesame seeds, for coating the falafel (optional)

1 litre olive, corn or sunflower oil, for shallow frying

freshly ground black pepper

for the hummus

2 x 400g cans chickpeas, drained

4 tablespoons Greek yogurt or cold water (for a dairy-free option)

150ml extra virgin olive oil, plus 2 tablespoons for drizzling

2 fat garlic cloves

juice of 1 large lemon (approx. 5 tablespoons), plus extra to taste

4–5 tablespoons tahini, according to taste

1½ teaspoons salt

¼ teaspoon freshly ground black pepper

1 teaspoon sumac, to garnish

serving suggestions

a handful of coriander, finely chopped (optional), Tahini Citrus Dressing (page 18), Tzatziki (page 92), Shredded Carrot, Parsley & Lemon Salad (page 148), Tabbouleh (page 68), pitta bread, crunchy leaves, olives, sliced tomatoes, spicy pickled peppers, sliced tomatoes and cucumber and gherkins

For the falafel, drain the chickpeas and put them in a food processor or blender, discarding the soaking water. Pulse for about 30 seconds until they form large crumbs, then add the onion, paprika, cumin, garlic, parsley, coriander, salt and freshly ground black pepper. Pulse again until the mixture resembles coarse breadcrumbs. Taste and add more seasoning to your liking. Finally, add the sesame seeds and pulse another couple of times. Chill for 20–30 minutes, this will allow the chickpeas to soak up the herb juices.

To make the hummus, put all the ingredients, apart from 6 whole chickpeas and the sumac, into a food processor and whizz until really creamy. Adjust to taste as necessary with more lemon, tahini or seasoning. Spoon into a serving dish. Pour a little olive oil on top of the hummus and use the back of a spoon to flatten it and spread over the olive oil. This does two things, makes it look glossy and attractive and protects the surface from becoming dry. Sprinkle sumac on top and garnish with the reserved chickpeas.

Remove the falafel from the fridge and create about 20 smallish balls or oval shapes about the size of a walnut. Pour the sesame seeds, if using, into a bowl and drop the falafel into the seeds one by one, turn them gently to coat all over and set aside.

Warm the oil in a frying pan or wok and when it is very hot add a few falafel balls one next to the other. Shallow-fry each side over a medium heat for 2 minutes. Drain on kitchen paper and serve warm, or at room temperature, with the hummus and a selection of accompaniments.

for spicy toasted pitta

These are great served with the hummus, tzatziki, Smashed Aubergine Relish or The Dip of Joy. Cut the pitta bread into strips about 4cm wide and split the pieces in half. Toss in a large bowl with plenty of olive oil, a little finely chopped chilli and garlic and salt and bake for 5 minutes in a very hot oven until crisp and lightly browned.

charred broccolini with lemon dressing, capers & pumpkin seeds

serves 6

Any member of the broccoli family will work for this salad. We like to use young broccoli florets with long stems when they are in season. If you are having a barbecue the broccoli is even better charred over an open fire.

600g broccolini and/or broccoli
1 tablespoon capers, in salt or in brine, rinsed well and drained
4 garlic cloves, left whole with skin on and lightly squashed
50g pumpkin seeds
3 tablespoons extra virgin olive oil
salt and freshly ground black pepper

for the dressing
juice and finely grated zest of 1 lemon
4 tablespoons extra virgin olive oil
1 tablespoon Dijon mustard
1 tablespoon raw mild honey or maple syrup (for a vegan option)

 If using maple syrup.

Preheat the oven to 200°C/gas mark 6. Line a baking tray with baking parchment.

If using broccolini, split the stalks in half lengthways from the ends to the start of the floret but do not separate the floret from the stem. For a whole head of broccoli, cut off just the woody end of the base by about 1cm. Divide the head and the stem into smaller florets with long stems. Each cut stem should be no more than 1cm wide or it will take too long to cook. Blanch the pieces in boiling salted water for 5 minutes or until the stalks are just tender, remove and drop into very cold water to stop them cooking.

Lay the broccolini, capers, garlic and pumpkin seeds onto the lined tray, drizzle over the oil and season well. Bake for 15–20 minutes or until lightly browned.

Meanwhile, whisk the dressing ingredients together in a jug. Slide the cooked broccolini from the baking parchment into a bowl and splash on the dressing. Serve hot or leave to come to room temperature.

shredded carrot, parsley & lemon salad

serves 6

This is one of the simplest salads in the book and probably the one we make most at home. We always seem to have carrots in the fridge, it is a go-to vegetable that the whole family eats and goes with so many dishes from Mediterranean and Asian to Japanese and South American.

3 medium carrots, coarsely grated
small handful of flat-leaf parsley, coarse stems removed, roughly chopped
1 tablespoon lemon juice
2 tablespoons extra virgin olive oil
1 teaspoon black onion seeds
small handful of coriander, coarse stems removed, roughly chopped (optional)
salt and freshly ground black pepper

Simply combine the ingredients in a bowl and season to taste. Serve straight away or keep in the fridge for up to 3 days. Serve at room temperature for the best flavour.

atsuko's soba noodle salad with sesame dressing

serves 6

Atsuko is a chef who teaches Japanese cookery at her London school Atsuko's Kitchen. She learned how to cook from her mother and grandmother at home in Kyushu, the southern island of Japan and her passion shows in her perfectly balanced recipes. This salad is served cold and has a wonderful texture from the nutty buckwheat noodles as well as the crunchy vegetables.

250g 100 per cent buckwheat soba noodles
150g green beans
4 spring onions, finely chopped
1 medium carrot, coarsely grated
½ cucumber, peeled, deseeded and cut into semi-circles

for the sesame dressing
3 tablespoons tahini
3 tablespoons mirin
4 tablespoons dark soy sauce or tamari
2 tablespoons rice vinegar
1 small garlic clove, finely chopped
2 tablespoons dashi stock or cold water
1 tablespoon black sesame seeds, to garnish

Cook the noodles in salted boiling water for 5 minutes or until just al dente. Drain and rinse them with your hands in a colander under cold water. Set aside to drain.

Cook the beans until just cooked but to the point when they retain a little crunch. Cool quickly under cold water. Set aside to drain.

Combine the dressing ingredients together in a blender or whisk by hand. A blender is ideal as you want the dressing to be smooth. If whisking by hand, make sure the garlic is cut very finely or crush it to a paste with the flat side of a knife.

Put the noodles, beans and remaining vegetables in a large dish and fold the dressing in, to coat. Garnish with the sesame seeds and serve straight away or keep in the fridge for up to 2 hours.

jeremy's silken tofu with chinese chives & toban jiang sauce

serves 4 as a starter, 6 as a main

This tofu salad is from Jeremy Pang who runs the School of Wok in London. I ordered the chilli bean sauce and black rice vinegar online but Chinese stores do stock them. The dressing also works on rice noodles and the salad. Serve with the Smashed Cucumber Salad (page 184).

for the dressing
3 tablespoons salted soy beans, soy bean paste or miso
2 tablespoons toban jiang (chilli bean paste) or other chilli paste
3 tablespoons light soy sauce
1 tablespoon chinkiang (black rice vinegar) or balsamic vinegar
1 tablespoon raw mild honey
3 tablespoons vegetable stock or water
1 tablespoon untoasted sesame or groundnut oil

for the tofu
350g pack firm silken tofu
a small handful of Chinese or ordinary chives, sliced into 3cm lengths
1 large handful of beansprouts, washed well
3 spring onions, finely sliced on the diagonal
⅓ English cucumber, peeled, deseeded and cut into bite-sized pieces
coriander sprigs, to garnish

To make the dressing, crush the salted soy beans into a rough paste (or use the soy bean paste or miso), then mix well with the remaining dressing ingredients.

Carefully open the pack of silken tofu, allowing the water to fall away, and transfer to the serving plate. Slice the block of tofu downwards into 3mm consecutive thick slices keeping the block shape intact. Put your hand gently on top and push the tofu down and to one of the shorter ends so that the slices fall slightly. This way you have more surface area to absorb the dressing.

Scatter the chives over the tofu and then add the beansprouts. Pour over the dressing, top with the spring onions and cucumber and garnish with the coriander.

6

hot pink beetroot & apple salad

vegetables à la grecque

ancient grain salad with seeds, nuts & roasted red onions

pomelo salad with coconut & lime dressing

moroccan crushed aubergine & tomato

fattoush

spiced green beans with tomatoes

quinoa kabsa with nut hashu

charred corn & avocado salad with chilli lime dressing

patatas bravas salad

asparagus & new potato salad with walnut oil vinaigrette

spicy tomato salsa

nepalese spicy onion & potato salad

kimchi

papi's & ranjit's shredded cabbage & carrot salad with peas

jewelled beetroot, orange, almond & dill salad

simple little sides

baby cress & toasted almond salad with buttermilk dressing

layered chickpea salad with tamarind sauce & yogurt dressing

ginger vichy carrot salad

avocado & orange salad

guacamole

jicama salad

smashed cucumber salad

cucumber raita

quinoa, courgette & corn salad

chopped salad of raw sprouts, chestnuts & radicchio

new potato salad with balsamic, sage & rosemary vinaigrette

pineapple & ginger salsa

fresh mango chutney

pico di gallo

a green salad

hot pink beetroot
& apple salad

serves 4–6

This ridiculously pink Swedish salad is lovely with pickled herrings, boiled eggs or cheese. If you want to save time buy ready-cooked beetroot, just not the ones in vinegar.

500g raw beetroot

2 crisp green eating apples, such as Granny Smiths

200ml soured cream

100ml mayonnaise, homemade (page 21) or shop-bought

1 tablespoon cider vinegar

1 shallot, finely chopped

100g gherkins, roughly chopped

1 tablespoon small capers, in salt or brine, rinsed well (optional)

salt and freshly ground black pepper

1 tablespoon finely chopped dill and/or a few crushed walnuts,
    to garnish

Put the whole, unpeeled beetroot into a medium pan of boiling water and cook for about 1 hour or until soft. Rub off the skins and trim the tops and bases. Cut into 2cm cubes and put into a serving bowl.

Core and cut the apples (we leave the skin on) into 2cm cubes and add to the bowl. Mix the remaining ingredients with the beetroot and apples, taste and adjust the seasoning, and serve garnished with dill or walnuts or both.

vegetables à la grecque

serves 4

This is Alain Roux's recipe. I was desperate to recreate the Champignons à la Grecque that I remembered from childhood holidays in Normandy. Vegetables prepared this way are a good accompaniment to any cold or hot fish and meat. You can vary the vegetables by using what is best in season but I prefer more button mushrooms because they remind me of the dish in my mind. Some of Alain's favourites are white and green asparagus spears, artichokes, baby fennel bulbs, cauliflower and broccoli florets, celeriac and young celery sticks.

Alain told me that this dish is best made a few hours or a day before and served with toasted crusty bread. I cook the beans for longer, if using, as Giancarlo has an aversion to squeaky beans, the Italians cook them for much longer than the French but I will let that argument stay between them!

for the à la Grecque dressing
½ teaspoon coriander seeds
½ teaspoon white peppercorns
50ml white wine vinegar
125ml olive oil
3 tablespoons concentrated tomato purée
75ml lemon juice
2 fat garlic cloves, crushed
1 small bouquet garni
50g caster sugar
pinch of salt

for the salad
1kg baby vegetables of your choice, trimmed (Alain uses
    8 baby fennel bulbs, 8 baby carrots, 8 baby courgettes,
    halved lengthways, few French beans, few radishes,
    8 small spring onions, 12 small button mushrooms)
2 tablespoons finely chopped flat-leaf parsley leaves, to garnish

Crush the coriander seeds and peppercorns using a pestle and mortar. Put the dressing ingredients plus 125ml water in a large pan over a low heat and simmer gently for 15 minutes, stirring occasionally with a whisk.

Meanwhile, blanch all the vegetables, except the mushrooms, separately in boiling salted water: allow 2 minutes for the fennel and carrots, about 30 seconds for the courgettes, French beans, radishes and spring onions. Drain and add the vegetables to the dressing. Add the raw mushrooms and simmer for 5 minutes.

Discard the bouquet garni, tip the vegetables into a serving bowl with the dressing and leave to cool. Season to taste with salt and pepper, scatter over the parsley and serve still warm or cooled to room temperature.

ancient grain salad with seeds, nuts & roasted red onions

serves 4–6

'Have you got indi grains?' said the American man named Neil sat next to me on the plane home. He realised I was writing about salads due to my open laptop and told me about how much he liked kasha (buckwheat), farro and freekeh. I hadn't heard them called indi grains before, but he said indi or heirloom grains were big in the States. He liked the texture, the fact they were 'toothsome' as he put it. So, Neil, here is your grain salad.

We wanted this to work as a side dish, to offer texture and satisfying carbs but not to stifle meat, fish or other vegetable main courses. If this is the main event then bump it up with feta, pomegranate seeds, fresh figs, eggs or whole cooked chickpeas. You could also serve it with Harissa Sauce (page 80), Hummus (page 146) or the Tahini Citrus Dressing on page 18. We have also tried this with crumbled crispy smoked bacon and chopped dates, or finely chopped preserved lemons and sun-dried tomatoes, both adding further layers of flavour.

200g ancient grains, such as freekeh, quinoa, farro, buckwheat or red or brown rice
1 large aubergine, cut into 1cm dice
2 large red onions, one cut into 1cm dice, one very thinly sliced
2 fat garlic cloves, skin on and lightly crushed
4 tablespoons rapeseed or extra virgin olive oil
75g mixture of almonds, pistachios, pine nuts, pumpkin or sunflower seeds
750ml groundnut oil
a large handful of flat-leaf parsley, roughly chopped
3 tablespoons dried fruit, such as blueberries, barberries, cherries, cranberries, currants or diced dried apricots
salt and freshly ground black pepper

for the dressing
juice of 1 medium lemon
5 tablespoons rapeseed or extra virgin olive oil

    If using quinoa, buckwheat or rice.

Preheat the oven to 200°C/gas mark 6.

Cook the grains according to the packet instructions, until tender. Drain and cool in a sieve.

Put the aubergine, diced onion and garlic in a bowl, season and coat with the oil. Spread the veg out on a baking tray and roast for 15–20 minutes until lightly browned and soft. Remove from the oven and set aside.

Meanwhile, toast the seeds and nuts on a separate tray in the oven for 5–7 minutes until just browned. Set aside to cool.

Heat the groundnut oil in a small saucepan until a small piece of bread sizzles in it. Deep-fry the sliced onion in the oil until crisp, it will take about 3–4 minutes – watch carefully as it burns easily. Set aside to drain on kitchen paper and season with a little salt.

Combine the dressing ingredients and season to taste. Assemble all the ingredients in a serving bowl, apart from the fried onion. Toss with the dressing and transfer to a serving dish. Top with the fried onion and serve straight away or refrigerate until you are ready. If the salad is chilled, let it come back to room temperature before serving.

pomelo salad with coconut & lime dressing

serves 4–6

This salad comes from The Market Restaurant and Cooking School in Hoi An where we learned to cook wonderful Vietnamese salads. Pomelo is a little like grapefruit, milder in flavour and with flesh that tears easily into shreds. Hunt them down in Asian stores as they make a refreshing and different salad. If you can't find one, this deliciously tropical dressing will work just as well on almost any shredded or diced raw vegetable, such as cabbage, Brussels sprouts, courgette and cucumber ribbons or with a little pink grapefruit instead. This salad can also be bumped up with prawns and chicken if you prefer.

for the dressing

4 tablespoons coconut milk

2 tablespoons lime juice

1 teaspoon raw mild honey (optional)

½ teaspoon chilli sauce, such as Sriracha

salt and freshly ground black pepper

for the salad

750ml sunflower or other seed oil, for frying

1 banana shallot or small onion, finely sliced

2 fat garlic cloves, finely sliced

1 pomelo

1 small white onion, finely sliced and soaked in cold water for
    15 minutes

a small handful of mint leaves

a handful of coriander or other Asian herb, such as Thai basil

¼–½ red or green hot chilli, according to taste, finely chopped

1 celery stick, cut in pointed stick batons

1 lemongrass stalk, very finely sliced

    If not using honey.

Combine the dressing ingredients and season to taste with a good pinch of salt and finely ground black pepper.

Heat the oil in a small pan over a high heat and fry the shallot and garlic until golden brown. This will only take a minute or two so don't let them burn. Drain on kitchen paper.

Peel and flake the flesh of the pomelo with your hands. Toss the remaining ingredients together, in a serving bowl, with the dressing and top with the deep-fried shallot and garlic.

moroccan crushed aubergine & tomato

serves 4

This unctuous mixture of smoky aubergine and spicy tomato is heavenly spread on bread, dolloped into lettuce leaves or served with grilled fish and meat. If you are making it in winter use 200g canned tomatoes, roughly chopped, instead of fresh ones and tomato purée.

2 large aubergines

3 tablespoons extra virgin olive oil, plus 1 tablespoon to garnish

4 round tomatoes, cut into 1cm dice

3 tablespoons tomato purée

2 tablespoons mild white or red wine vinegar

1 fat garlic clove, finely chopped

1 heaped teaspoon ground cumin

1 teaspoon salt

1 heaped tablespoon finely chopped coriander

1 heaped tablespoon finely chopped flat-leaf parsley, plus a few leaves to garnish

Preheat the oven to 220°C/gas mark 8.

Prick the aubergines in four places with a sharp knife then put on a baking tray and roast for 45 minutes until completely burnt. They should be charred to the point of the skin flaking and turning white. Alternatively, you can burn the pricked aubergines with a cook's blowtorch or over an open flame by carefully holding them and turning with a pair of metal tongs. It will take about 5 minutes to blister the skins.

Leave the aubergines to cool and then peel away and discard the skins. This is easier under running water if you have burnt them over a flame. Roughly chop the flesh and set aside in a bowl.

Pour the oil into a large frying pan and add the chopped tomatoes. Cook for a few minutes until they have softened then add the remaining ingredients with the aubergines. Use a large wooden spoon or spatula to turn the ingredients so that they are well combined. Partially cover the frying pan with a lid and cook for about 20 minutes over a low heat, this will thicken the mixture to a paste as the water evaporates.

Taste and adjust the seasoning as necessary. Serve warm or at room temperature with a swirl of olive oil and a little flat-leaf parsley on top.

fattoush

serves 6–8

This famous Lebanese salad has been popular for centuries and is a great way to use up pitta bread that is past its best. The vegetables should change seasonally and they are usually torn or cut into bite-sized pieces rather than finely chopped as in a tabbouleh. This is wonderful with any Middle Eastern spread or simply as a side to roast or barbecued meats. The pungent citrus flavour of the sumac adds a mouthwatering sour note to the dish.

Amal Alquahtani showed me the way to toast bread for this salad; it makes all the difference and helps use up leftover pitta bread. You can keep the pieces bigger and use them for dips too.

1 shallot, cut into thin rings

4 brown or white pitta breads

¼–½ red chilli, finely chopped

1 garlic clove, finely chopped

4 tablespoons olive oil

1 head of Romaine lettuce, cut into 3cm strips.

3 tomatoes, cut into 3cm chunks or 12 cherry tomatoes, halved

1 cucumber, peeled and cut into 1cm dice

3 radishes, sliced

a small handful of mint leaves, woody stems discarded

a small handful of flat-leaf parsley, roughly chopped and firmer stems discarded

1 teaspoon black onion seeds (optional)

salt and freshly ground black pepper

for the dressing

1 garlic clove, finely chopped

juice of 1 lemon

100ml extra virgin olive oil

3 tablespoons pomegranate molasses

1 red wine vinegar

1 teaspoon sumac, plus extra to serve

1 teaspoon sugar (optional)

Preheat the oven to 200°C/gas mark 6.

Soak the shallot rings in cold water for 20–30 minutes to weaken their flavour, then drain well.

Cut the bread, with scissors, into 3cm strips and split open. Tear each strip into three and toss in a bowl with chilli, garlic, olive oil and salt and pepper. Lay onto a baking tray and cook for 10–15 minutes until browned. Remove from the oven and leave to cool.

Mix all the dressing ingredients together and season to taste. Add a little sugar if it is too tart.

Put all the salad ingredients in a large bowl, including the cooled bread, and toss together gently with the dressing. Scatter a good pinch of sumac over the top and serve.

spiced green beans with tomatoes

serves 4–6

This is another of our friend Amal's recipes from Kuwait although there are variations of this dish all over the Middle East and the Mediterranean. Don't gasp at the amount of olive oil, she used a lot more and it doesn't go to waste as you can soak up the juices with bread at the end. The beans are cooked slowly in tomatoes and olive oil, rendering them soft and lightly spiced by the garlic and chilli. This is usually a side dish and can be served warm or at room temperature but I could eat a bowl of these on their own or with fried eggs.

1 medium red or white onion, finely chopped

7 tablespoons extra virgin olive oil

2 garlic cloves, finely chopped

¼–½ teaspoon dried chilli flakes, according to taste

325g flat, runner or French green beans, trimmed

250g tomatoes, roughly chopped

2 heaped tablespoons tomato purée

salt and freshly ground black pepper

a squeeze of lemon juice, to serve

a little sumac, to garnish

Fry the onion in the oil in a large frying pan, with a lid, over a low heat for about 10 minutes until soft. Add the garlic and chilli flakes and continue to fry for a further 2 minutes over a low heat and then add the beans, tomatoes, purée, 100ml water and seasoning. Partially cover with the lid and cook the beans until soft, depending on their size this will take 20–30 minutes.

Taste the sauce and add more seasoning or chilli as necessary. Squeeze over a little lemon juice, scatter over some sumac and serve or leave to cool and serve at room temperature.

quinoa kabsa with nut hashu

serves 6–8

This lightly spiced dish is based on a rice dish called Kabsa from Kuwait and was taught to us by our friend Amal. Traditionally a whole chicken is boiled to make stock and then the rice is cooked in it with spices. The chicken is then roasted and served with the rice. If you like to make stock from scratch do try this method or use the poached chicken for the Coronation Chicken with Lychees (page 72) or the Shredded Chicken and Cabbage Salad (page 81). If you are catering for vegetarians, use vegetable stock instead.

We have used quinoa but rice or couscous works just as well. Keep it simple but do add roasted vegetables or salad leaves if you like.

for the stock

1 litre chicken stock

5 cardamom pods, lightly crushed

1 large cinnamon stick

1 teaspoon ground coriander

½ teaspoon ground black pepper

3 cloves

1 teaspoon ground cumin

1 teaspoon ground turmeric

3 garlic cloves, whole but lightly crushed

1 small bunch of coriander or flat-leaf parsley stalks

pinch of saffron strands

for the hashu

1 shallot, finely chopped

1 garlic clove, finely chopped

2 tablespoons extra virgin olive oil

a large handful of pine nuts, almonds or pistachios or a mixture
   of all 3

50g sultanas, soaked

a pinch of saffron strands

pinch of crushed dried lime or fresh lime zest

a splash of rose water (optional)

salt and freshly ground black pepper

for the quinoa

250g quinoa, rice (for a gluten-free option) or couscous

100g dried organic apricots

seeds from 1 pomegranate

a handful of coriander leaves, roughly chopped

a handful of flat-leaf parsley leaves, roughly chopped

Put the stock ingredients in a medium pan, bring to the boil and reduce to a simmer for about 20 minutes, over a low heat.

Meanwhile, prepare the hashu. Gently fry the shallot and garlic in the oil with 3 tablespoons of water for about 10 minutes until soft. Add the nuts, drained sultanas, pinch of saffron, lime zest, seasoning and rose water, if using, and stir through. Cook for 5 minutes and set aside.

Taste the stock and add salt to your liking. If the flavours are not strong leave it to cook for a further 10 minutes. When the stock is ready, strain it and discard the flavourings.

Cook the quinoa according to the packet instructions, using the stock instead of water. Drain and set aside to cool.

Combine the quinoa with the apricots, pomegranate seeds and herbs and serve with the hashu spooned over the top.

  If using quinoa or rice.

charred corn & avocado salad with chilli lime dressing

serves 6–8

We love the flavour of lightly blackened corn which transforms a bland cob into a caramelised flavour reminiscent of homemade popcorn, giving a sweet, nutty flavour to this salad. If you don't have black beans, any cooked, canned variety will do. When squeezing limes, pop them in the microwave for 15–20 seconds and they will be much easier to juice. We have given the instructions for grilling indoors but if you have a barbecue going charring the cobs is quick and gives a lovely smoky flavour.

for the salad

4 corn on the cob, husks and silk removed

1 small red onion or 5 spring onions, finely chopped

400g can black beans

250g cherry tomatoes, halved

1 red or yellow pepper, deseeded and cut into 1cm dice

1 avocado, peeled, stoned and cut into 1cm dice

a small bunch of coriander, roughly chopped

for the dressing

6 tablespoons fresh lime juice, from 3–4 limes

5 tablespoons extra virgin olive oil

1 garlic clove, roughly chopped (optional)

½ teaspoon dried oregano

½ teaspoon ground cumin

⅛–¼ jalapeño chilli or other chilli, according to taste, finely chopped

½ teaspoon salt

freshly ground black pepper

Preheat the grill to medium-hot.

Lay the corn on a rack, put them under the grill and let them brown, watching them carefully and turning frequently so that they don't blacken to blistering – this will take a few minutes. You want them rich brown with a few black tinges rather than looking like they have been up the chimney. Set aside to cool.

Meanwhile, put the onions in a bowl of cold water to reduce their strength. Let them sit for about 10 minutes, then drain in a sieve and set aside.

Drain and rinse the beans in a sieve, under cold water, to rinse well. Set aside.

When the corn is cool, hold each cob upright in a large bowl and slice downwards near the core with a sharp knife to cut the kernels off the cob in strips. If the corn stays in strips break them up into kernels. Transfer the corn to a serving bowl and add the remaining ingredients.

Combine the dressing ingredients in a jug or bowl. Taste and adjust the seasoning as necessary and pour over the salad. Toss gently and serve.

patatas bravas salad

serves 6–8

This is based on a popular Spanish recipe from Catalan chef and teacher Carolina Català-Fortuny for fried potatoes with hot spicy sauce. A rather touristy, but nonetheless delicious, addition to this is a few heaped tablespoons of mayonnaise mixed with a finely chopped garlic clove. This should be dolloped over the top of the brava sauce or served separately. Our boys say it is better with fried or roast potatoes but we like it with boiled new potatoes. In the photo we used boiled new potatoes and then crisped up the outside by frying them but really any cooked potatoes will do. This is also excellent with barbecued meat and fish.

1.2kg new or old potatoes, whole and unpeeled

4 tablespoons extra virgin olive oil

salt and freshly ground black pepper

for the brava sauce

3 tablespoons extra virgin olive oil

1½ tablespoons smoked sweet paprika

1 tablespoon red wine vinegar

200g canned tomatoes, roughly crushed

pinch of cayenne pepper or chilli powder or dash of Tabasco
    sauce (optional)

for the garlic mayonnaise

1 small garlic clove, finely chopped

125ml mayonnaise, homemade (page 21) or shop-bought

a small handful of flat-leaf parsley, stalks removed, leaves roughly
    chopped, to garnish

Boil the potatoes in salted water until just cooked but don't let them overcook and break up. Drain as soon as they are done and set aside to cool a little.

Meanwhile, make the sauce. Heat the olive oil over a low heat in a saucepan, add the paprika and fry for a couple of minutes, stirring constantly or it will burn. Add the vinegar and cook for a further 2 minutes until it has evaporated almost completely. Then add the tomatoes and a pinch of salt and cook over a medium heat until the sauce thickens, stirring frequently. Break up the tomatoes with a potato masher. It will take roughly 15 minutes. Add the cayenne, chilli or Tabasco sauce, to taste, towards the end. Blitz with a hand-held electric blender to get a smooth sauce.

Mix the garlic and mayonnaise together in a small bowl and set aside.

Heat the olive oil in a large non-stick frying pan and when hot add the potatoes, breaking them up with your hands. Season and fry over a medium heat for about 10 minutes until browned. Depending on the size of your pan you may need to do this in batches.

Carolina suggests pouring the brava sauce just over the top of the hot potatoes, not completely covering them. This way everyone can choose what size potato they want, with a lot or just a little sauce. Spoon over the mayonnaise and scatter with the parsley to serve.

asparagus & new potato salad with walnut oil vinaigrette

serves 6

This makes a lovely side dish for a summer buffet or any roast chicken or fish when local asparagus are in season. Alternatively, add soft boiled quail's eggs to the salad and serve as a starter or main course. We like to use the leftover oil from cooking the vegetables in the tray to make the vinaigrette, adding a little walnut oil to enrich the flavour.

500g new potatoes, washed

12 quail's eggs (optional)

250g asparagus, woody ends discarded

150g baby leeks or spring onions, tough green ends discarded

5 tablespoons extra virgin olive oil

a large handful of firm lettuce leaves, such as Baby Gem or
   Romaine, roughly torn and bitter ribs removed

a handful of flat-leaf parsley, roughly chopped

1 quantity of Classic Vinaigrette (page 20) instead of the olive oil in
   the recipe use the cooking oil from the tray and walnut oil

salt and freshly ground black pepper

    If not using eggs.

Cook the potatoes in their skins, in plenty of boiling water, until tender. Drain.

If using eggs, gently lower them into boiling water and boil for 2 minutes. Remove from the water and immediately plunge them into cold water, crack the shells straight away to stop a blue ring appearing. Peel them when cool enough to touch and set aside.

Preheat the oven to 180°C/gas mark 4.

Put the asparagus and leeks on a baking tray, toss with the oil to make sure they are all covered and season. Cook for 12–15 minutes or until lightly browned and tender. Remove from the oven and set aside to cool.

Put the lettuce, flat-leaf parsley, vegetables and dressing in a serving bowl and gently toss to combine. Taste and adjust the seasoning as necessary and serve the halved eggs on the side, if using.

spicy tomato salsa

serves 8–10

Every time our good friend Margaret Boynton stays with us we ask her to make her spicy salsa to eat with corn tortillas crisps. She grates mature Cheddar cheese over them and grills them for a few minutes in the oven before eating them warm with the salsa. Raised in Texas, now living in Georgia, she knows a thing or two about customizing Tex-Mex-style salsa and uses canned tomatoes when fresh aren't available. The recipe makes a generous amount but it keeps in the fridge for up to 4 days. The chia seeds are my addition to thicken the sauce.

6 spring onions, roughly chopped

½ teaspoon garlic powder or granules or 1 fat garlic clove, finely chopped

2 x 400g cans Italian whole or chopped plum tomatoes

⅛–¼ jalapeño or red chilli, according to taste, roughly chopped

½ teaspoon smoked chipotle chilli powder (optional)

1 teaspoon ground cumin

1 tablespoon red wine vinegar or 2 tablespoons lime juice

a small handful of fresh coriander, roughly chopped

1 tablespoon chia seeds (optional)

salt and freshly ground black pepper

Drain the tomato juice from the cans (save it for a Bloody Mary), then put everything into a food processor and whizz briefly until the onions are chopped small.

nepalese spicy onion & potato salad

serves 6–8

This recipe was given to me by our friend and Nepali-Indian author Prajwal Parajuly. Nepalese food is traditionally hot and spicy – this recipe is normally finished with tempered (fried) chillies and fenugreek seeds, making it very hot and slightly bitter. We have reduced the amount of chilli for our Western palate and replaced the fenugreek with black onion seeds. We love to eat this dish with halved boiled eggs and mango chutney or Cucumber raita (page 172) or the Tandoori Salmon & Prawns on page 112.

1 large cucumber

1 red onion, thinly sliced into half moons

500g potatoes, one type only or a mixture of sweet, white or new, peeled and cut into 2cm cubes

3 tablespoons sesame seeds

juice of 1 large lemon, plus extra to taste

4 tablespoons olive or seed oil

½–1 red or green chilli, according to taste, roughly chopped

1 teaspoon black onion seeds

½ teaspoon Szechuan peppercorns, ground

½ teaspoon ground turmeric

1 teaspoon chilli powder

a large handful of coriander, tough stalks removed, roughly chopped

a large handful of mint leaves, tough stalks removed, roughly chopped

salt

Peel the cucumber and halve lengthways. Scoop out the seeds with a spoon and discard them. Cut the cucumber into batons about 1cm wide and 4cm in length. Put them into a colander and scatter with 1 teaspoon of salt. This will bring out the moisture and ensure they offer a crunch to the salad. Set aside for 30 minutes.

Soak the onion slices in cold water to reduce their strength.

Meanwhile, cook the potatoes in plenty of boiling salted water until tender and just cooked but not falling apart. Drain and set aside to cool a little.

Toast the sesame seeds in a dry frying pan until they start to pop and become golden brown. Remove from the heat and pour onto a plate to cool.

Wash the cucumber slices and drain well, pour into a large mixing bowl. Drain the onions and add to the bowl with the potatoes and lemon juice.

Warm the oil in a pan and when hot fry the chilli until it starts to brown. Add the remaining spices and fry for a further minute, stirring constantly. Pour this oil (called tempering) over the salad, scatter over the fresh herbs and sesame seeds and mix together. Taste and add more salt or lemon juice as necessary. Serve at room temperature.

kimchi

makes about 1.25kg

Korean kimchi was traditionally a way to preserve cabbage to eat throughout winter. It is hugely popular in Korea and each household has their preferred way to make it. It is thought to be very good for you as it contains naturally occurring probiotics, such as lactobacillus, antioxidants and fibre as well as vitamins and minerals.

Our Korean neighbour Hye Yeong gave us this recipe. She eats fresh kimchi from the day of making it or 6-month-old kimchi with rice topped with sesame seeds, in stir-fries or with pork dishes.

Often kimchi is made with sweet, glutinous rice powder made into a porridge and cooled, which helps to stick the paste to the vegetables but we can't get hold of that easily so usually make it without. You can use a variety of vegetables as well as the cabbage or simply keep it as cabbage only.

1kg napa cabbage (about 1–2 cabbages, depending on their size)
6 tablespoons fine or coarse sea salt, plus up to 2 teaspoons, to taste
1 medium white onion
2 teaspoons finely grated fresh ginger
2 fat garlic cloves
2–3 tablespoons Korean red pepper powder or dried chilli flakes, according to taste
1–2 tablespoons sugar, according to taste (optional)
2 teaspoons Korean fish sauce (optional)
200g vegetables, such as mooli (long white radish), carrot or radish, cut into julienne strips
5 spring onions, quartered lengthways and cut into 5cm lengths or a large handful of chives
rice and toasted sesame seeds, to serve

Cut off the woody ends from the cabbages and split them in half lengthways. Cut out a triangle to remove the remaining tough stems. Cut each half into 5 pieces across the leaves so that you are left with lots of pieces of cabbage about 6cm x 6cm. Wash the cabbage and drain, then mix in the 6 tablespoons of salt using your hands. Leave the cabbage to salt for 4 hours, turning it every hour.

Meanwhile, use a blender to make a spice paste from the onion, ginger, garlic, red pepper powder, sugar and fish sauce, if using.

When the cabbage has salted, wash it very well in two changes of cold water. To do this use two bowls, one filled with the cabbage and water and the other empty. Lift the cabbage out of the water with your hands letting the salty water drip away. Fill the second bowl with the clean water and repeat the process – there should be a hint of salt left to the taste. If it is very strong wash again. Leave it to drain in a colander for a further 30 minutes.

Now combine the pepper paste with the cabbage leaves, other vegetables and spring onions, using your hands and making sure they are well covered. Pack into a 3-litre lidded plastic container, pressing it down so there is not too much air inside. Close the lid and leave it to sit for a day at room temperature.

Move the container to the fridge. It will ferment slowly. Press it down every day for the first week. It can be eaten straight away or left for up to 6 months in the fridge. The flavour will mature slowly. When you want to eat it, remove what you need and press the remaining kimchi down so that it is covered with the juices. Serve with rice and toasted sesame seeds.

papi's & ranjit's shredded cabbage & carrot salad with peas

serves 4–6

Shanthini from Papi's Pickles, a co-operative Indian catering company in London, told us about this salad. It's called Poriyal in southern India and is hugely popular as it is quick and easy and contains turmeric, which gives it antibacterial properties. It is crunchy with the cabbage and nuts and bursts with citrus and chilli flavours. Any leftovers can be fried and supplemented with beaten eggs for breakfast the next day. The same method is used for finely sliced runner beans, stringless green beans and other varieties of beans and beetroot. Quite often yogurt is added to make a pickle known as Pachadi.

Homemade Gujarati cabbage salad, known as Sambharo, is almost identical and was taught to us by our friend Ranjit Cheema. It is a healthy choice as it is cooked quickly so is still crunchy, and served at room temperature. It can be served with plain rice for a wonderfully complete vegetarian meal. Peanuts, sultanas or chickpeas can be added to the dish to make it more substantial.

We have combined these dishes into one (see photo on page 143) and hope not to have upset either friend!

100g frozen peas

350g white cabbage (about ½ medium cabbage)
3 tablespoons sunflower or vegetable oil
½–1 green chilli, according to taste, sliced into rings
1 tablespoon cumin seeds
½ teaspoon black onion seeds
½ teaspoon black mustard seeds
1 teaspoon salt (optional)
½ teaspoon ground turmeric
2 sprigs curry leaves (optional)
50g peanuts (optional)
350g carrots, coarsely grated
50g sultanas (optional)
juice of ½ lemon
a small handful of coriander, tough stems discarded and roughly chopped
chapatti or paratha, to serve

    If served without chapatti or paratha.

Cook the peas until just tender in boiling water, drain and set aside. Prepare the cabbage by discarding the outer leaves and cutting it into slices about 3mm thick with a large, sharp knife. Now lay a few of these onto a board on top of one another and slice down thinly to make long thin strips, the size of matchsticks.

Heat the oil and the chilli and seeds, in a large non-stick frying pan for a minute or two until the seeds pop, stir in the salt, turmeric and curry leaves, if using. Add the peas and ensure they are well coated in the oil and spices. Add the cabbage and stir constantly, over a high heat, for about 4–5 minutes until the cabbage strips become soft like al dente pasta.

Toast the peanuts in a dry frying pan over a medium heat until lightly browned. Toss regularly. Remove from the pan and set aside to cool.

Add the carrots, peanuts and sultanas, if using, and cook for about 3 minutes until the carrots have softened.

Add the lemon juice, keeping the heat high and stirring constantly for a minute or two to incorporate the flavours. Scoop into a dish and scatter over the chopped coriander. Serve with chapatti or paratha.

jewelled beetroot, orange, almond & dill salad

serves 4–6

Ruby beetroot, amber carrots and shards of golden almonds make this intensely colourful combination very good for you, especially as they are raw and packed with vitamins. The sweet orange dressing and delicate fronds of dill give the salad a real punch of flavour. Serve it with any of the Middle Eastern or Mediterranean salads or alongside grilled salmon or mackerel, roast chicken or simply boiled eggs.

for the dressing

1 teaspoon finely grated orange zest

100ml freshly squeezed orange juice (approx. 2 small oranges)

3 tablespoons extra virgin olive oil

salt and freshly ground black pepper

for the salad

a small handful of flaked almonds

2 small raw beetroots, peeled and coarsely grated

2 medium carrots, peeled and coarsely grated

1 orange, peeled and segmented, each segment halved

a small handful of golden sultanas

a small handful of dill, stems removed and torn into fronds

seeds of 1 pomegranate

1 teaspoon black onion seeds (optional)

Prepare the dressing by reducing the orange zest and juice in a small frying pan over a medium heat. Leave it to bubble gently until reduced by about half. Leave to cool. When cool, mix with the oil, salt and pepper. Taste and adjust the seasoning as necessary.

Toast the almonds in a dry non-stick frying pan over a medium heat until lightly browned, toss frequently to prevent them burning.

Put the salad ingredients in a bowl, reserving a few dill fronds and almonds to garnish. Toss together with the dressing before transferring to a serving dish. Top with the reserved dill and almonds.

variations

For a more Middle Eastern flavour, change the dill to flat-leaf parsley and add ground cumin and 1 tablespoon of pomegranate molasses.

baby cress & toasted almond salad with buttermilk dressing

serves 6

This is a wonderfully crunchy side salad or starter with roast chicken, poached or hot-smoked salmon or boiled eggs. The dressing can be made up to two days ahead and any leftover buttermilk can be used up in a smoothie. We use celery from our garden – it has a very strong flavour when it is home-grown, so if you are using shop-bought add as many leaves as you can from the bunch; they have a great deal of flavour and are frequently under-used. If you sprout your own seeds or lentils by all means substitute those for the cress.

for the dressing

1 tablespoon finely chopped chives

1 tablespoon finely chopped flat-leaf parsley

1 tablespoon finely chopped tarragon leaves

75ml mayonnaise, homemade (page 21) or shop-bought

100ml buttermilk or 80ml crème fraîche diluted with 20ml milk
or soured cream

1 tablespoon lemon juice

1 teaspoon raw mild honey (optional)

1 small garlic clove, finely chopped

3 tablespoons extra virgin olive oil

salt and freshly ground black pepper

for the salad

75g flaked almonds

300g soft salad leaves, such as lamb's lettuce or butterhead lettuce

2 pots sprouted cress (about 60g after cutting) or other sprouted
seeds

2 celery sticks and a handful of leaves, finely sliced

3 teaspoons pink peppercorns

Combine the dressing ingredients and stir well. Season to taste and pour into a jug to serve. Store in the fridge if not using straight away.

Toast the almonds in a dry frying pan over a medium heat until lightly browned. Toss regularly. Remove from the pan and set aside to cool.

Mis the salad ingredients in a large serving bowl, then scatter over the pink peppercorns, lightly crushing them by hand as you drop them over. Serve with the dressing on the side.

layered chickpea salad with tamarind sauce & yogurt dressing

serves 6–8

This dish is based on the popular Indian and Pakistani street food salad Chana chaat, with chickpeas, yogurt, tamarind dressing and crunchy topping. Indian cookery teacher Zahda Saeed helped us get the flavourings right and showed us how to stir-fry the base then layer the salad. Her family eats this as a side dish at a barbecue or dinner but it is substantial enough to stand on its own or with boiled eggs. It can be served hot or prepared the day before and served at room temperature. Chaat powders are spice mixes and along with tamarind sauce are available in Asian stores or most supermarkets. Taste the chaat powders before adding, however, as they can be very salty.

for the yogurt dressing
200g natural yogurt
½ teaspoon garam marsala
½ teaspoon ground cumin
20g coriander, finely chopped
salt and freshly ground black pepper

for the salad
3 tablespoons olive oil
1 heaped teaspoon cumin seeds
1 heaped teaspoon chaat powder
1 heaped teaspoon garam marsala
1 heaped teaspoon cumin powder
1 heaped teaspoon ground coriander
½–1 teaspoon salt, according to taste
¼ teaspoon ground turmeric
½–1 green chilli, according to taste, finely chopped
400g can chickpeas, drained
1 large tomato, cut into 1cm slices
1 medium potato, roughly chopped (optional)
1 red pepper, deseeded and thinly sliced into long strips
1 green pepper, deseeded and thinly sliced into long strips
1 medium red onion, finely sliced
juice of ½ small lemon
tamarind sauce, to serve
a few coriander or mint leaves, to garnish
50g crunchy topping, such as Bombay mix

Mix the dressing ingredients together in a bowl and season to taste.

Next, stir-fry the vegetables. Get the oil really hot, add the cumin seeds and allow them to start spitting and sputtering then add the remaining spices and chilli. Stir in the chickpeas and coat them with the spicy oil. Add the remaining vegetables and stir through. Reduce the heat and continue to cook for 5 minutes so that the vegetables have just started to soften but retain some bite. Add a squeeze of lemon juice and mix well.

Serve straight away with the yogurt dressing dolloped over, a few splashes of tamarind sauce, the coriander or mint leaves and the crunchy topping.

ginger vichy carrot salad

serves 4–6

My mother always cooked carrots Vichy-style, minus the ginger, when I was growing up. It is a classic French way from the town of the same name, and uses the famous Vichy water. It was one of my jobs in the kitchen to make sure the carrots didn't burn. As a large family we had a lot of fun in the kitchen preparing food together and as I regularly got distracted the carrots often became a little more caramelised than my mother would have liked! Now I add ginger to the recipe plus a couple of toppings. This is a lovely accompaniment to roasts, a good starter or vegetarian main course.

350–400g medium or baby carrots with green tops
25g butter
25g fresh ginger, peeled and sliced
salt and freshly ground black pepper

for the ginger yogurt
20g fresh ginger, peeled and very finely chopped
1 tablespoon extra virgin olive oil
6 tablespoons Greek yogurt

for the carrot top crunch
2 tablespoons flaked almonds
a small handful of carrot tops, if you have them
a small handful of flat-leaf or curly parsley

Remove the tops of the carrots and reserve. Split the medium carrots in half lengthways, leave the baby ones whole. Boil the kettle. Put the carrots, butter, ginger slices, a good pinch of salt and freshly ground pepper plus 600ml water from the kettle into a medium saucepan and bring to the boil, partially covered with a lid. Reduce the heat to a simmer and continue to cook for 15–20 minutes until the carrots are cooked through.

When the carrots are cooked lift them out with a slotted spoon and keep warm in a serving dish in a low oven. Reduce the sauce, with the lid off, until you are left with about 3 tablespoons of buttery sauce. Watch the liquid carefully as you don't want the liquid to boil away completely but you do want it to thicken as it reduces.

For the ginger yogurt, fry the ginger in the oil over a medium heat in a small frying pan for 5 minutes. It shouldn't burn but it should release the flavour into the oil. Remove from the heat and set aside to cool. Mix with the yogurt and add salt to taste.

Toast the almonds in a dry frying pan over a medium heat until lightly browned. Toss regularly. Remove from the pan and set aside to cool.

Chop the reserved carrot tops, parsley and almonds together on a chopping board using a large knife. Season well.

Pour the reduced buttery sauce over the carrots, scatter over the almonds and serve the yogurt on the side, to dollop on.

avocado & orange salad

serves 4–6

This salad was given to me by keen cooks and Sydney residents Robin and Chris Doucas, who kindly told me their favourite Australian salads.

We like the simplicity of this dish and the combination of the three main ingredients is really all you need with your best single-estate extra virgin olive oil. Use the best oranges in season; blood oranges look beautiful. Sweet red onions work just as well as spring onions. Robin enjoys this salad with seafood dishes either before, during or after the main dish or simply as a sports snack that perks up your energy without weighing you down.

3 sweet oranges
3 ripe, but firm, avocados
3 spring onions, finely sliced
5 tablespoons best extra virgin olive oil
a squeeze of lemon juice, to taste
salt and freshly ground black pepper

Peel the oranges and divide into segments over a bowl to collect the juice. Peel and stone the avocado and cut into slices.

Arrange the avocado slices, orange segments and onions in a serving bowl. Mix any collected orange juice with the oil, lemon juice and seasoning and pour over the salad. Serve straight away or leave for up to 1 hour.

guacamole

serves 4–6

Guacamole should be made out of perfectly ripe avocados, preferably the dark green, bumpy-skinned Hass variety as they have a good flavour and creamy texture. Try guacamole spread on toast, with fish, chicken, carrot sticks, on its own for a snack or heaped onto halved boiled eggs.

Traditionally guacamole is made in a molcajete, a three-legged volcanic stone pestle and mortar. At home it is easy to crush the avocados with a fork, cut the garlic minutely by hand and chop the coriander with scissors. Add or leave out the chilli as you wish, but taste it first, and remember the heat is in the pith and not the seeds. Alternatively, add a tablespoon of Pico di Gallo (page 188) to the mashed avocados instead of the other ingredients.

3 ripe Hass avocados, peeled and stoned
juice of 2 limes
½–¾ teaspoon salt
a small handful of coriander, finely chopped
⅛–¼ jalapeño chilli or ¼–½ red chilli, according to taste, finely chopped
1 garlic clove, finely chopped
1 medium round tomato, diced

Mash the avocados with a fork in a medium bowl and add the remaining ingredients, taste and adjust the salt and chilli for the balance of seasoning and heat. Guacamole will keep in the fridge, covered, for a couple of days.

jicama salad

serves 4

Jane Milton is a good friend and wonderful food writer. She collects recipes on her travels and introduced us to jicama, a round, brown root vegetable. It has a texture somewhere between a water chestnut and a crisp apple with a subtle banana flavour. Jicama is widely used in Chinese cooking as well as South American dishes and is also known as a yam bean or Chinese turnip. You can find them in Asian stores and they are worth hunting down for their delicious texture and flavour. If you can't find it, Jane suggests using a crisp, green eating apple such as Granny Smith's instead.

This is one of her favourite Mexican salads from her book *The Practical Encyclopedia of Mexican Cooking*; it's delightfully crisp and sweet and good with barbecued meat or fish.

1 small red onion, halved and finely sliced
juice of 2 limes
2 small oranges
1 medium jicama (about 450g)
½ English cucumber
½–1 red fresno, red or green chilli, according to taste

Put the onion slices and lime juice in a bowl and leave to soak while preparing the other ingredients.

Cut the peel and the white pith from the oranges and then, using a small, sharp knife, cut between each segment to free the flesh and leave all the pith together. Squeeze the pith to extract any remaining juice. It is a good idea to segment oranges over a bowl to catch the juice and add this to any obtained by squeezing the pith.

Peel the jicama, rinse in cold water. Cut into quarters and then finely slice into a serving bowl. Cut the cucumber in half lengthways and use a teaspoon to scoop out the seeds, cut into 3mm slices and add to the bowl. Remove the stalk from the chilli and slit and remove the seeds with a sharp knife by gently scraping. Chop it finely and add to the salad.

Mix the orange segments and juice with the onion and add to the jicama, cucumber and chillies. Chill for at least an hour before serving. It will keep for 2–3 days in the fridge.

smashed cucumber salad

serves 4

Our Chinese bank manager Laura Lin-Wilkes suggested we include this recipe. We hadn't heard of it before but asked Asian cookery expert Jeremy Pang for help. It is now one of our son Giorgio's favourites; he loves cucumber, Chinese food and the idea of hitting vegetables with a rolling pin, so it is a winner all round! Do get the timing right for this – it should only marinate for 30 minutes and it is better to eat it soon after. This is a refreshing salad with Jeremy's Silken Tofu with Chinese Chives & Toban Jiang Sauce (page 149), poached fish or any Chinese food.

1 English cucumber
5 spring onions, thinly sliced
1 teaspoon black sesame seeds

for the pickling liquid
1 teaspoon Chiu Chow chilli oil or 1 teaspoon seed oil and
 ½–1 teaspoon chilli flakes, according to taste
1 tablespoon tahini
4 tablespoons chinkiang (black rice vinegar) or balsamic vinegar
2 tablespoons raw mild honey or maple syrup (for a vegan option)
½ teaspoon salt
1 tablespoon light soy sauce or tamari (for a gluten-free option)
15 Szechuan peppercorns, crushed
1 garlic clove, finely sliced

    If using maple syrup and tamari.

Slice the cucumber in half lengthways then remove the core with a teaspoon. Cut each length in half again lengthways so you have 4 long quarters. Slice each length into large 3cm chunks. Put them into a food bag and seal it closed. Using a rolling pin, lightly crush the cucumber by bashing it around but try to keep the cucumber pieces more or less whole but bruised. (Be careful not to pierce the bag.)

Mix the pickling liquid ingredients together, with 2 tablespoons hot water, in a bowl, stirring well until the tahini has dissolved. Pour it into the bag with the cucumber. Seal again and put in the fridge for 20–30 minutes but no longer or it will become soft. Remove from the fridge and discard three-quarters of the liquid. Put the cucumber into a serving dish, top with the remaining sauce and scatter over the spring onions and sesame seeds.

cucumber raita

serves 4–6

Use as an accompaniment to the Layered Chickpea Salad with Tamarind Sauce & Yogurt Dressing (page 180), curries or chicken salad. You can add milk or water to make it runnier. It will keep in a sealed container in the fridge for up to a week. If it separates, mix it through before serving.

1 teaspoon cumin seeds

½ cucumber, coarsely grated

400g thick natural yogurt

½ fine salt

1 teaspoon raw mild honey (optional)

½ teaspoon black pepper

a small handful of mint, finely chopped (optional)

chilli powder and chopped coriander, to garnish

Roast the cumin seeds in a dry, small frying pan over a medium heat, until lightly browned and smelling strongly – don't let them burn. Set aside to cool.

Put the grated cucumber in a sieve to drain, for at least 10 minutes.

Mix all the ingredients together, in a serving bowl, and garnish with chilli powder and coriander.

quinoa, courgette & corn salad

serves 4–6

This simple combination of three main ingredients is just lovely. With a glut of courgettes, that frequently seem to morph into marrows during the night, we are always looking for ways to use them up. This is a great side to a main event or can be made into the star with the addition of avocado slices, toasted nuts, feta or shavings of Parmesan.

200g quinoa or other grains, such as farro, freekeh or brown rice

2 medium courgettes or a small marrow (about 350g total weight), cut into 1cm dice

2 tablespoons olive oil or coconut oil

3 tablespoons extra virgin olive oil

1 cooked corn on the cob, kernels scraped off or 200g canned sweetcorn

a handful of flat-leaf parsley, tough stems discarded, roughly chopped

salt and freshly ground black pepper

    If using quinoa or brown rice.

Cook the grains according to the packet instructions, until tender.

Meanwhile, fry the courgette cubes in the olive or coconut oil for 5 minutes, tossing regularly or until lightly browned but still firm. Set aside.

Drain the grains and toss with the olive oil, courgettes, corn and seasoning in a serving bowl. Leave to cool to room temperature and toss in the parsley just before serving.

chopped salad of raw sprouts, chestnuts & radicchio

serves 6

Winter and summer versions of this variable salad of finely chopped vegetables are fun to invent. I first saw this at the Wild Rabbit in Kingham. It contains raw Brussels sprouts, carrots and chestnuts, combining colour and texture in a wonderful tangy mustard dressing. They nearly always have a chopped salad on the menu, changing the ingredients according to the season. Although this salad is all about the crunch, it is a good idea to include something soft, such as chestnuts or a cheese, for instance a good Cheddar or Manchego. We enjoy our version on its own or in a collection of other European salads.

1 small red onion, finely chopped
125g Brussels sprouts, shredded
125g carrots, finely chopped
125g radicchio, finely chopped
125g kohlrabi, finely chopped
2 celery sticks and a few leaves, finely chopped
1 eating apple, such as Cox's, finely chopped
a small handful of chives, finely chopped
a handful of cooked chestnuts (vacuum-packed are ideal),
    crumbled or finely chopped
75g Cheddar cheese, finely cubed
1 quantity of Honey Mustard Dressing (page 19)
salt and freshly ground black pepper

Soak the onion in cold water for 20–30 minutes, then drain well.

Combine the onion with the remaining ingredients and the dressing in a serving bowl. Taste and adjust the seasoning to your liking.

new potato salad with balsamic, sage & rosemary vinaigrette

serves 4–6

This rich herby dressing is from our friend Wendy Holloway, in Rome, who uses it frequently at her cookery school. In summer she loves this dressing on roasted peppers or fresh borlotti beans, and in winter it's great on boiled potatoes or roasted vegetables. Perfect for barbecues and accompanying grilled meats.

1.2kg new or old potatoes, peeled and cut into 3cm cubes
1 garlic clove, finely chopped
1 small red onion, finely chopped
10cm sprig rosemary, stalk discarded and leaves finely chopped
a few sage leaves, stalks discarded
5 tablespoons extra virgin olive oil
1 tablespoon balsamic vinegar
salt and freshly ground black pepper

Cook the potatoes in plenty of boiling salted water until tender.

Meanwhile, make the dressing by mixing the remaining ingredients together in a bowl. When the potatoes are tender, drain and, using tongs, put them into a serving dish crushing them lightly with the tongs. Pour over the dressing and gently toss the potatoes so they are all covered. Serve straight away or leave to cool to room temperature. They will keep well in the fridge for a couple of days but do let them come to room temperature before serving or pop them quickly in the oven to heat through.

pineapple & ginger salsa

serves 4–6

Originally from South America, the pineapple was brought via the Carib Indians to the Caribbean where it was discovered by Christopher Columbus in 1493. Over the years it became a symbol for sailors to say they were back home. They left one outside their homes to say 'I'm back, come and see me!'. And to this day it has become a symbol of hospitality. Pineapple salsa is often served with Mexican as well as Caribbean foods. It is spicy and sweet and pairs well with grilled prawns, fish, ham, and spicy sausages.

½ small red onion, finely chopped
500g ripe pineapple, peeled and cut into 5mm dice
½ red pepper, deseeded and cut into 5mm dice
½–1 red chilli, according to taste, finely chopped
2 teaspoons finely grated fresh ginger
juice of 1 lime
small handful of coriander, coarse stems removed, finely chopped
salt and freshly ground black pepper

Soak the onion in water while you prepare the other ingredients.

Toss the pineapple and pepper in a serving bowl with the drained onion and the remaining ingredients. Season to taste and serve straight away or keep in the fridge for up to a day.

fresh mango chutney

serves 6

We love this quick chutney served on the side of any Indian, South East Asian or South American salads, it adds colour and the sweetness of the mango calms down any guests suffering from the chilli heat!

1 mango, cut into 1cm slices
1 tablespoon finely chopped coriander leaves
2 teaspoons finely grated fresh ginger
juice of ½ lemon or 1 lime
¼–½ green or red chilli, according to taste, finely sliced
salt

Combine the ingredients in bowl, adjust the seasoning to taste and serve.

pico di gallo

serves 4–6

This south American spicy salsa is simply gorgeous and can be used in so many ways – as a topping for bruschetta with a spicy twist, served with grilled fish and meats or piled into tacos.

200g flavourful tomatoes, either one kind or a mixture of large, medium or cherry, roughly chopped
½ shallot or 2 spring onions, finely chopped
1 garlic clove, roughly chopped
¼–½ jalapeño or other chilli, according to taste, roughly chopped
a small bunch of coriander, roughly chopped
juice of 1 lime
salt and freshly ground black pepper

Mix the ingredients together in a large bowl and taste. Adjust the seasoning as necessary. Serve straight away or within a couple of hours if chilled.

a green salad

serves 6

What is a green salad? It is easier to say what it shouldn't be. It shouldn't be an undressed bowl of bitter lettuce such as frisee accompanied by some sliced cucumber and a little bitter green pepper. Hard to eat, with no flavour, providing nothing but colour.

Giancarlo says it is a British thing that we have to have a green vegetable or a salad with every meal. It drives him and his fellow Italians mad when we have a dressed salad with a bowl of hot pasta. The Italians, French and Japanese eat salad before a meal to open up the appetite. if you are going to eat it as a side, it should not dominate the main course, it should complement it. So in terms of the dressing choose something mild, such as the one below, a simple blend of lemon juice and a good but gentle extra virgin olive oil.

Our perfect green salad could be as straightforward as a butterhead lettuce fresh from the garden. A quick wash and rinse followed by a dousing in our Classic Vinaigrette (page 20) and we are in heaven. For a side with interest to go with a steak for example, add a variety of leaves, fresh herbs, finely cut green vegetables, such as cucumber, courgettes, pepper, peas or mangetout and the Honey Mustard dressing (page 19). For a salad to go with South East Asian dishes try the Sesame Ginger Soy Dressing (page 18). For added texture see the suggestions photographed on page 9 such as toasted nuts, seeds or the sourdough crumbs such as those on page 134 to give it crunch. To make this more filling add protein such as sliced avocado, crumbled feta, mozzarella or torn chicken. A green salad need never be boring again.

200g mild-flavoured lettuce, such as Butterhead, Baby Gem, Romaine, bitter stalks trimmed away

½ cucumber, peeled and cut into batons

1 celery stick, thinly sliced on the diagonal

25g strong-flavoured leaves, such as mustard, rocket, dandelion, watercress or sprouted seeds such as cress, amaranth or sprouted lentils

15g assorted leaves of parsley, coriander, chives, chervil, sweet cicely, wild fennel, mint, basil

for the dressing

1 tablespoon lemon juice

2 tablespoons extra virgin olive oil

salt and freshly ground black pepper

Assemble the salad ingredients in a large bowl. Shake the lemon juice and olive oil together in a jar with the seasoning. Pour over the salad, toss gently with tongs or two spoons (or your hands) and serve straight away.

on the
sweet side

roast black fruit salad with amaretto & cashew lime cream

strawberry, pistachio & mint salad with rose water cream & meringue

blackstrap molasses & tahini with dates, nuts, bananas & apples

kiribath with pear, cashew & apricot salad

raspberries & redcurrants with whipped ricotta, lemon curd & ginger crumbs

stuffed dates with feta & mint

labneh

roast figs & apricots stuffed with granola, cinnamon & honey labneh

roast black fruit salad with amaretto & cashew lime cream

serves 4–6

For a brief time cherries cross in season with blackberries and plums. Dark fruits such as these are full of antioxidants and blend well together on the plate. Depending on the sweetness of the fruit adjust the honey to your liking, you may not need any. Large juicy blackberries are better for roasting than hard wild ones.

You need a powerful stick or high-speed blender to achieve a smooth cashew cream or it will remain slightly grainy. We love the nutty flavour and texture and it is a good vegan alternative for those who are dairy free. The fruits are also good with Whipped Coconut Cream (page 34) or Lemon Crème Fraîche (page 79).

for the cashew lime cream

200g cashews, soaked in cold filtered water for 2 hours

zest and juice of 1 lime

1–2 tablespoons raw mild honey or maple syrup, according to taste

for the fruit salad

600g mixed fruit, such as cherries, plums, blackberries, blackcurrants and blueberries

1–2 tablespoons raw mild honey, maple syrup or caster sugar (optional), according to taste

5 tablespoons Amaretto, Grand Marnier or other liqueur or sweet wine of your choice

      If using maple syrup or sugar.

To make the cashew lime cream, drain the cashews and combine with the remaining ingredients and 100–120ml water, in a blender, adding a little more water as necessary to obtain a smooth cream that will easily drop from a spoon. Sweeten to taste with honey, maple syrup or sugar. The cream will keep for 3 days in the fridge in a sealed container.

Preheat the oven to 180°C/gas mark 4.

Cut the plums, if using, into small wedges about the size of the blackberries so that they have the same cooking time. Cut the cherries in half and remove the stones. Leave the remaining fruits whole. Drizzle over the honey, maple syrup or sugar, if using, and roast the fruit for 15–20 minutes or until just softened. Add the liqueur and roast for a further 5 minutes. Remove from the oven and leave to cool to room temperature. Serve with the cashew lime cream.

strawberry, pistachio & mint salad with rose water cream & meringue

makes 50 small meringues 4cm across and 2–3cm tall

This stunning party piece is sure to delight – summer strawberries are piled onto whipped rose water cream and broken meringues. It's easy to assemble and you can decorate it with edible fresh rose petals, pistachios and mint. It will also work in individual glasses.

We use Welsh rose water, which is absolutely lovely and available online. Rose water is also available from Middle Eastern stores and supermarkets but they do vary. Expect to pay more for a good one and it will make all the difference.

There are various methods of making meringue but we find the one below the most useful. It follows the Swiss method and is more robust than others when making flavoured meringues or using in a semifreddo.

for the meringues
150g egg white (about 5 egg whites)
300g caster sugar

for the coulis
250–350g strawberries, hulled and cut in half
2–3 tablespoons caster sugar

for the cream
60g icing sugar
600ml whipping cream
4–5 tablespoons rose water

to serve
300g strawberries
a handful of small mint leaves
25g pistachios, peeled
a handful of pink edible rose petals, from organic roses
    or wild dog roses

Put the egg whites and three-quarters of the sugar into a mixing bowl and stir together. Put this over a pan of boiling water making sure that the water does not touch the bowl. Whisk using an electric mixer until the mixture comes up to 45°C on a thermometer or until it starts to become glossy and very thick. Remove from the heat and put into a food mixer with a whisk attachment or use an electric mixer and whisk until it doubles in size. While it is running, add the remaining sugar little by little.

Preheat the oven to 110°C/gas mark ¼. Line two baking trays with baking parchment.

Pipe or spoon the meringues 4cm across and 2–3cm tall onto the lined trays. Cook for 30–40 minutes or until they are light to the touch, lift off easily and are crisp on the outside and slightly soft on the inside. If you like your meringues brittle, leave them in the oven for a further 15 minutes. Leave to cool.

To make the coulis, boil the strawberries and sugar for 15 minutes until the fruit has softened and reduced in volume. Strain through a sieve and cool.

For the cream, whip the icing sugar and cream together until stiff and beat in the rose water to taste.

To serve, pile the meringues, cream and strawberries onto a serving plate (or into individual glasses) and top with the mint, pistachios, rose petals and coulis.

blackstrap molasses & tahini with dates, nuts, bananas & apples

serves 6

We were told about this unusual mixture from Yehia El Alaily, an Egyptian photographer. He showed us his beautiful photograph of a bowl of tahini swirled with molasses which he had with a cup of black coffee. We experimented pouring it over different fruits and this is the best combination. It is also really delicious on toast scattered with sesame seeds. Dukka is an Egyptian mixture of nuts, seeds and spices normally served with bread and oil, in this case Susie, our food stylist made a sweet version, which we loved.

for the sweet dukka

50g nuts and seeds, such as pistachios, almonds, walnuts, sesame seeds

½ teaspoon black peppercorns

1–2 teaspoons brown sugar (optional), to taste

for the fruit

6 bananas, sliced lengthways

2 red-skinned apples, cored cut into pointed batons

1 pear, cored and cut into pointed batons (optional)

juice of ½ lemon

6 Medjool dates, pitted and quartered lengthways

2 tablespoons clear honey

4 tablespoons tahini

3 tablespoons blackstrap molasses

Preheat the oven to 180°C/gas mark 4. Line a baking tray with baking parchment.

Toast the nuts on a baking tray for about 8–10 minutes or until lightly browned, and shake the tray halfway through. Add the seeds halfway through. Pour the nuts and seeds from the paper onto a plate to cool.

Make the dukka by grinding the peppercorns to a coarse powder using a pestle and mortar. Add the nuts and sugar, to taste, and grind again to make a coarse crumble. Set aside.

Put the bananas, apples and pear, if using, onto a serving plate and squeeze over the lemon juice. Scatter over the dates. Drizzle with a little honey and dust with the dukka. Swirl the tahini and molasses together in a bowl and serve on the side for guests to help themselves.

kiribath with pear, cashew & apricot salad

serves 4–6

This Sri Lankan combination of sweet coconut rice and sour dried fruits in honey is heavenly comfort food on a cold day. For the dried fruits you can use apricots, mango, pears, sultanas, dates, cherries or cranberries. Kiribath can also be left to cool and cut into squares and eaten with mango purée and fresh fruits or simply on its own with a cup of coffee. As with all rice dishes, rice should be cooled quickly and put into the fridge within an hour of cooking. This is Manjula Samarasinghe's recipe, she serves it after a hot Sri Lankan curry.

125g basmati rice or Asian red rice

6 dried apricots

4 dried pear halves

50g cashews or pistachios

4 Medjool dates, pitted

400ml coconut milk

1 teaspoon vanilla extract

2 teaspoons raw mild honey or maple syrup (for a vegan option), plus 2 tablespoons for serving

    If using maple syrup.

Soak the rice in cold water for 30 minutes. Soak the apricots, pears and nuts in hot water from a kettle for 20 minutes, while you prepare the dried fruit salad.

Cut the dates into 5mm pieces and put into a bowl, if they are very sticky do this with a wet knife.

Remove the fruit and nuts from the water and cut the fruits into 5mm pieces and add to the dates.

Drain the rice and put it into a pan with 200ml of water and cook, according to the packet instructions, until it is just done, then add the coconut milk a little at a time until you achieve a pourable consistency and continue to cook for a further 5 minutes, adding the vanilla and honey or maple syrup to taste.

Remove from the heat and pour into small glasses to serve. Top with the dried fruit pieces and a drizzle of honey or maple syrup. Serve straight away.

raspberries & redcurrants with whipped ricotta, lemon curd & ginger crumbs

serves 6

Simple and effective, this quick-to-make dessert is ideal in summer when raspberries and redcurrants are bursting with sweetness. We love the slightly tart ricotta with the sweet lemon curd rippled through it. We make our own gluten-free ginger biscuits but do buy your favourite brand to crumble over for an instant finish.

150ml whipping cream
250g ricotta, drained
100g lemon curd
300g raspberries
50g redcurrants or other red berries, such as loganberries
2–3 ginger biscuits, to decorate

  If using gluten-free ginger biscuits.

Use an electric whisk to whip the cream and ricotta into soft peaks. Spoon this onto a serving platter and swirl through the lemon curd. Scatter the berries on top and crumble over the biscuits. This will sit happily in the fridge for a couple of hours if you want to prepare it in advance.

stuffed dates with feta & mint

makes 10

This is such a simple little recipe and it really is delicious. It is from our chef friend Moustafa who has six restaurants in Cairo and loves to promote Egyptian food. I serve these at the end of a meal with a coffee but they are equally good for breakfast with a juice as the natural sugar in the dates gives you a burst of energy.

10 Medjool dates
50g feta cheese, crumbled
1 tablespoon chopped mint leaves

Make a lengthways cut in the dates and open them up leaving the two halves attached with a hinge. Remove the stones. Mix the feta with the chopped mint and stuff the dates. Close up the dates and serve chilled or at room temperature.

labneh

makes approx. 200g

Strictly speaking labneh is not a cheese but it resembles one. It is in fact strained yogurt that tastes like cream cheese. If made from fresh, live yogurt, labneh is better for you than most pasteurised cream cheeses as the probiotics are still active. It is easy to make and very adaptable. Use it like cream cheese or alter the taste with herbs and spices. Keep it in the fridge for up to 5 days.

for salted labneh
450g thick natural sheep's, goat's or cow's milk yogurt
1 teaspoon salt

for sweet labneh
450g thick natural sheep's, goat's or cow's milk yogurt
2–4 tablespoons raw mild honey, added according to taste
½ teaspoon ground cinnamon

Cut a large square of muslin about 75cm square. Lay this into a sieve and pour over a kettle full of boiling water to sterilise it. Squeeze it out and lay it into a bowl.

Scoop the yogurt into the centre of the cloth. Pull up the outer edges and tie it around the neck with string. Hang it up to drain with a bowl underneath it. The longer you leave it the drier and firmer the yogurt will become. Leave it for up a day until it stops dripping for a consistency like cream cheese, just 4–5 hours will do for soft labneh. You can discard the watery residue although this is live whey and can be used as a starter for sauerkraut, kimchi or for scones.

Scrape out the labneh into a bowl and add either the salt or honey and cinnamon depending if on which labneh you are making.

savoury variations
Try chopped chives, flat-leaf parsley, lemon zest, garlic or chilli. A drizzle of good olive oil over the surface adds a glossy appearance, a little more flavour and stops it forming a crust.

roast figs & apricots stuffed with granola, cinnamon & honey labneh

serves 4–6

These have a distinctly wintery feel about them. If you don't want to make labneh and can't buy it easily from a Middle Eastern stores use thick Greek yogurt instead. The filling is so delicious it is a good idea to use up any leftover (or I actually make double the quantity) to make Granola Bites (page 32).

for the stuffing
50g Medjool dates (approx. 3 dates), stones removed before
   weighing
25g yellow or green sultanas, soaked overnight in cold water and
   drained
50g dried apples, apricots or pears
2 teaspoons vanilla extract
1–2 teaspoons ground cinnamon
100g nuts, such as walnuts, pine nuts, pecans, almonds, soaked
   overnight in cold water and drained
25g pumpkin seeds, soaked overnight in cold water and drained

6 fresh apricots (it doesn't matter if they are not completely ripe)
6 small fresh figs

Preheat the oven to 150°C/gas mark 2.

Make the stuffing by whizzing the dates, sultanas, dried apples, vanilla, cinnamon and nuts in a food processor until they form a rough paste. Remove from the processor and stir in the pumpkin seeds.

Halve and stone the apricots and make two cuts in the top of each fig and push them open. Push a walnut-sized piece of stuffing into each fruit and lay onto a tray. Bake for 15–20 minutes or until the fruits have softened and are lightly browned. Serve with the sweet Labneh (see opposite).

resources

The Guildhall Library
www.cityoflondon.gov.uk/things-to-do/guildhall-library/Pages/default.aspx
Charles Dowding has great books and courses on how to grow salad; see
www.charlesdowding.co.uk
For nuts, spices, seeds and loads more try www.healthysupplies.co.uk
Paolo Arrigo at Seeds of Italy is where we get all our seeds at seedsofitaly@gmail.com
For great shops with really knowledgeable staff for healthy products try
www.revital.co.uk
Go to the Japan Centre on Shaftesbury Avenue for products. White miso is eaten in
the west of Japan. www.japancentre.com/en/stores
Clearspring are great for Japanese, macrobiotic and organic supplies,
find stockists at www.clearspring.co.uk
For the stranger ingredients in the book, Sous Chef is a brilliant online distributor
www.souschef.co.uk
For Welsh rose water got to www.petalsofthevalley.co.uk for the best sweet-smelling,
addictive rose water – available with a spray attachment.
Hard-to-find ingredients can usually be sourced at www.melburyandappleton.co.uk

Cookery schools and teachers

Zhada Saeed teaches her wonderful Indian food at www.authenticindianfood.com
Sara Mittersteiner runs a vegan catering business called Pomodoro E Basilico, which
includes supper clubs and private catering but is now mostly street food markets!
Follow her on Instagram at pomodoro_e_basilico
Jeremy Pang teaches amazing Asian at www.schoolofwok.co.uk
Atsuko teaches Japanese home style cooking at www.atsukoskitchen.com/catering
Silvia Nacamulli is a brilliant teacher of Italian and Jewish cookery
www.cookingforthesoul.com
Wendy Holloway – learn Italian food in Rome with www.flavorofitaly.com
Carolina Català-Fortuny – teacher and caterer of super Spanish food
spooninhand@gmail.com
La Cucina Caldesi Ltd – come to us to learn Mediterranean dishes, especially
everything Italian, and now salads! www.caldesi.com

My favourite places to while away my days when I should be writing

Tieghan Gerard who creates her inspired blog at www.halfbakedharvest.com
Food52.com – a huge site full of the latest recipes and a source of wonderful
inspiration
Another favourite blog to watch www.thekitchn.com

index

Acknowledgements

Thank you so much to:-

Anne Head whose frustration at finding salad recipes was the inspiration for this book and the 'spice ladies' for the best time in Morocco – all this grew from that weekend!

Sheila Abelman, our literary agent for putting the plan into action.

Kyle Cathie – thank you for believing in the idea of the wonderful world of salad.

Vicky Orchard and Amberley Lowis for bringing it all together.

Helen Cathcart for such beautiful photography and tireless energy.

Susie Theodorou, Camilla Baynham for bringing my recipes to life with your amazing styling and the ever-patient Nicole for all her washing up.

Louise Leffler for her lovely book design.

Linda Berlin for the perfect props.

Thank you Jamie Macdonald for enabling us to have the best week ever in NY.

To all our amazing friends that helped us research, test (sometimes the same dish over and over again, I know!), eat and develop recipes. You were so patient with us and gave us so much time – thank you to Karin Piper, Amal Alquahtani, Linda Hutchings, Anne Hudson, Louise Ford, Carly and Robbo Roberts, Susie Jones, Karen Courtney, Sally Dorling, Joe Mosse, Reiko Hara, Margaret and Mike Boynton, Ranjit Cheema, Manjula Samararasinghe and Stefano Borella.

And thank you to the happy tasters for being polite when faced with yet another new salad to try: Sian and Steve, Ian and Carrie, Philip, Giorgio and Flavio.